SEVILLE

UPDATED BY
FIONA FLORES WATSON

www.bradtguides.com

Bradt Guides Ltd, UK
The Globe Pequot Press Inc, USA

Bradt GUIDES
TRAVEL TAKEN SERIOUSLY

This is
Seville

Seductive, sun-baked and hedonistic, the city of Seville, capital of Andalucía, in many ways embodies the romance of the region. This is the brightest star in the Andalucian tapas firmament and has a post-Reconquest architectural heritage unmatched in the south, from the evocative Alcázar to the giant Gothic cathedral.

Seville was the focal point of the Golden Age of Spanish painting, and many of the country's most memorable canvases are to be seen here, in the excellent galleries and in countless Baroque churches, built to represent a Catholic faith. From the same source sprang the city's famed Semana Santa processions, which are the largest and best known of the solemn Easter celebrations in Spain. Hard on its heels though, the riotous Feria de Abril exemplifies many features of the other side of the Andalucian character.

But as many as the temptations of Seville are, the rest of this landlocked province also commands attention. The agricultural settlements of the fertile Guadalquivir valley present a great contrast to the sophisticated bustle of the capital. Carmona was an important fortified town for several different civilisations; further east, Écija has an extraordinary number of Baroque churches, while the town of Osuna has many elegant Renaissance mansions.

Seville gets powerfully hot in summer, and locals either hightail it for the beach or head north to the cooler Sierra Morena. Cazalla de la Sierra is one of the best spots to base yourself here, a peaceful whitewashed town with plenty of not-too-strenuous walking in the vicinity.

Best of
Seville

❶ Cathedral, Seville city

Seville's cathedral is a marvellous Gothic edifice on a monumental scale that imposes by its sheer bulk. Its numerous side chapels are a wonderful repository of art, while its Moorish-Renaissance tower, the Giralda, and the weather vane atop it are famous city landmarks. Page 11.

❷ Real Alcázar, Seville city

Built mostly after the Reconquest in Gothic, Mudejar and Renaissance styles, this handsome palace and fortress of the kings of Castile boasts a series of handsome chambers featuring beautifully detailed stucco work, calligraphy and arches, and a sumptuous walled garden. Page 15.

❸ Parque María Luisa, Seville city

The 1929 Ibero-American Exhibition was held here and left a legacy in a series of striking buildings centred around the enticing Parque María Luisa. Particularly notable are the huge semicircle of the Plaza de España, the upmarket Alfonso XIII hotel and the city's archaeological museum. Page 25.

4

⑥ Casa de Pilatos, Seville city

This ducal mansion on the edge of atmospheric Barrio Santa Cruz is one of Seville's most impressive aristocratic homes. A blend of Renaissance and *mudéjar* architecture, it has an elegantly classical feel and a stunning central courtyard. Page 32.

④ Triana and La Macarena, Seville city

These working-class barrios are imbued with the true essence and character of Seville, and make fantastic places for a stroll. Reverence for Semana Santa sculptures, flamenco, local markets and tile workshops, and a palpable sense of tradition and history make these places special. Pages 28 and 34.

⑤ El Ayuntamiento, Seville city

Seville's town hall is set between two plazas in the heart of town. It was built in two distinct phases and features stunning Renaissance stonework. It's well worthwhile taking the guided tour of its interior to appreciate the impressive carved function rooms. Page 31.

⑦ Museo de Bellas Artes, Seville city

The city's main art gallery has a wonderful collection of Spanish painting in a characterful former monastery. Local boy Velázquez is represented, but the gallery is particularly notable for its brilliant works by the giants of Seville's Golden Age of art: Zurbarán and Murillo. Page 33.

8 Itálica

Wander the ruins of what was once one of the Roman Empire's major cities, a large complex that was originally built as a rest-and-relaxation base for troops. It's easily accessed on local buses from Seville and can be combined with a visit to an interesting nearby monastery. Page 37.

9 Sierra Morena

The wooded hills of the northern part of Seville province can come as a cool relief after the baking heat of its central plains. Cazalla de la Sierra is the best base for exploration, a whitewashed town that offers walking trails and local liqueurs. Page 54.

10 Carmona

Atmospheric Carmona is an easy day trip from Seville and offers a pleasantly compact old centre, ideal for strolling. The highlight is the Roman necropolis: descending into its enormous patrician tombs is a thrill; some of them preserve wall paintings. Page 56.

Seville city

The capital of Andalucía was accurately described in the 16th century as having 'the smell of a city and of something undefinable, of another greatness'. While the fortunes of this one-time mercantile powerhouse have waxed and waned, its allure has not; even within Spain its name is spoken like a mantra, a word laden with sensuality and promise. Delving beyond the famous icons – the horse carriages, the oranges, the flamenco, the haunting Semana Santa celebrations – you find a place where being seen is nothing unless you're seen to be having fun, a place where the ghosts of Spain walk the streets, be they fictional, like Don Juan or Carmen, or historical, like Cervantes, Columbus, Caesar or Joselito.

Seville has an astonishingly rich architectural heritage within its enormous old town, still girt by sections of what was once Europe's longest city wall. The bristling Moorish tower of the Torre del Oro, the Baroque magnificence of numerous churches, the gigantic Gothic cathedral and the *mudéjar* splendours of the Alcázar: these and much more are ample reason to spend plenty of time in Seville – you could spend weeks here and not get to see all the sights.

But the supreme joy of the city is its tapas. They claim to have invented them here, and they are unbeatable; you'll surely find that your most pleasurable moments in this hot, hedonistic city come with glass and fork in hand.

Essential Seville city

Most sights are in the old town, one of Europe's largest historic city centres. Because much of it is pedestrianised, walking is the best way to get around. Contactless payments can be used on public transport.

Bus

To avoid the fierce summer heat, take one of Seville's air-conditioned city buses. Bus C5 does a useful circuit around the centre, including La Macarena. A single ticket costs €1.40 (€5 for a day ticket).

Metro

Seville has a metro, www.metro-sevilla.es, with only one line operational so far. Line 1 links the satellite towns of Mairena de Aljarafe and Dos Hermanas with the centre. Useful stops are Prado de San Sebastián for the bus station; Puerta de Jerez near the cathedral and Barrio Santa Cruz; Plaza de Cuba for southern Triana and the Feria; and Nervión, the modern shopping area near Sevilla FC's football stadium. However, most of the interesting parts of tourist Seville are not covered by the network. A single costs €1.35 for short journeys (€4.50 for a day ticket).

Taxi

Taxis are a good way to get around. An illuminated green light means they are available, and they are comparatively cheap. Uber and Cabify also operate here.

Tram

Seville's tram line zips between Plaza Nueva and Luis de Morales in Nervión, via the cathedral, Puerta de Jerez and Prado de San Sebastián (for the bus station). In late 2026, the final planned stop, Santa Justa train station, is due to open. A single ticket costs €1.40.

When to go

Peak season in Seville, when prices are notably higher, is March to May, with the most pleasant weather and the two major festivals, Semana Santa and the Feria de Abril. Summer is a quiet time as temperatures can be almost unbearable (hitting the mid-40s°C in recent years); autumn is a good time to visit, and winter is much milder here than elsewhere in Europe.

Time required

At least three days to see the main sights.

Weather Seville

Month	High	Low	Rainfall
January	15°C	6°C	73mm
February	17°C	6°C	59mm
March	20°C	9°C	38mm
April	23°C	11°C	51mm
May	26°C	13°C	36mm
June	32°C	17°C	9mm
July	36°C	20°C	1mm
August	36°C	20°C	5mm
September	32°C	18°C	25mm
October	26°C	14°C	60mm
November	20°C	10°C	84mm
December	16°C	7°C	95mm

Plaza del Triunfo s/n, T954-214971, www.catedraldesevilla.es. Mar-Oct (exact dates vary according to daylight saving time) Mon-Sat 1100-1900, Sun 1200-1900; Oct-Mar Mon-Sat 1100-1800, Sun 1430-1900; Jul and Aug (except 17 and 25 Jul) Mon 1030-1600, Tue-Sat 1030-1800, Sun 1400-1900; you can prebook a free visit on Sun 1630-1730. €13; €5/€4 audio guide/app. Buying tickets online in advance is cheaper and avoids queues.

Seville's bases of ecclesiastical and royal power, the cathedral and Alcázar face each other across the sun-beaten Plaza del Triunfo, once just inside the city's major gateway. They're both heavily visited, and with good reason: you should give plenty of your time to visit either and linger in a quiet corner while the tourist groups surge past. In the squares around, horse carriages sit under the orange trees ready to trot visitors around the sights of the city.

The fall of Seville to the Christians in 1248 was an event of massive resonance: it represented the breaking of the backbone of Muslim Spain. After a while, at the beginning of the 15th century, the Castillians decided to hammer home the point and erect a cathedral over the mosque (which they had been using as a church), on a scale that would leave no doubts.

Santa María de la Sede is the result, which contains so many riches that most of its chapels and altars could have been tourist attractions in their own right; there are 80 of them.

Several Moorish elements were happily left standing; the city's symbol, the superb Giralda tower, is the most obvious of these. Originally the minaret of the mosque, it was built by the Almohads in the late 12th century and was one of the tallest buildings in the world in its day. Although rebuilt by the Christians after its destruction in an earthquake, its emblematic exterior brick decoration is true to the original, although the famous weather vane atop the structure (El Giraldillo) is not.

Approaching the cathedral, try to start from Plaza de San Francisco, behind the Ayuntamiento. Taking Calle Hernando Colón, another Moorish feature will soon become apparent – the Puerta del Perdón gateway, with fine stucco decoration and a dog-toothed horseshoe arch. Turning left and walking around the whole structure will let you appreciate the Giralda and the many fine 15th-century Gothic doorways. You enter either via the Puerta del Lagarto, by the Giralda (online tickets) or the Puerta de San Cristóbal/del Príncipe (in-person tickets).

It's impossible to list here all the works of artistic merit contained within the huge five-naved space. Entering through Puerta de San Cristóbal, the first chamber is a small museum with several excellent pieces including a head of the Baptist by Juan de Mesa; a Roldán Joseph and Child; a San Fernando by Murillo; and a Zurbarán depicting the Baptist in the desert.

Around the chapels

Once into the cathedral proper, after catching your breath at the dimensions and the pillars like trunks of an ancient stone forest, do a circuit of the chapels. Don't

Seville

LA CARTUJA

To Hospital de las Cinco Llagas

Basílica de la Macarena

Santa Marina

LA MACARENA

Convento de Santa Paula

Plaza del Pumarejo

San Luis

Santa Paula

La Alhóndiga

Recaredo

Plaza Ponce de León

Plaza Padre Pías

San Esteban

Jerónimo Córdoba

Santiago

Casa de Pilatos

Museo del Baile Flamenco

CENTRO

Ayuntamiento

Plaza Alfalfa

Plaza Encarnación

Plaza Villasís

Sierpes

Alameda de Hércules

Plaza San Martín

Plaza Zurbarán

Plaza del Duque

Jesús del Gran Poder

San Lorenzo y Jesús del Gran Poder

Plaza San Lorenzo

Museo de Bellas Artes

La Magdalena

Plaza de Armas

Río Guadalquivir

Pasarela de la Cartuja

Monasterio de la Cartuja & Centro Andaluz de Arte Contemporáneo

Camino de los Descubrimientos

To Isla Mágica & ⑧

Américo Vespucio

To Huelva

Capilla de

Puente Cristo de la Expiración (Puente del Cachorro)

Marqués de Paradas

Menéndez Núñez

To Santa Justa train station, airport, Córdoba & Málaga

Bradt

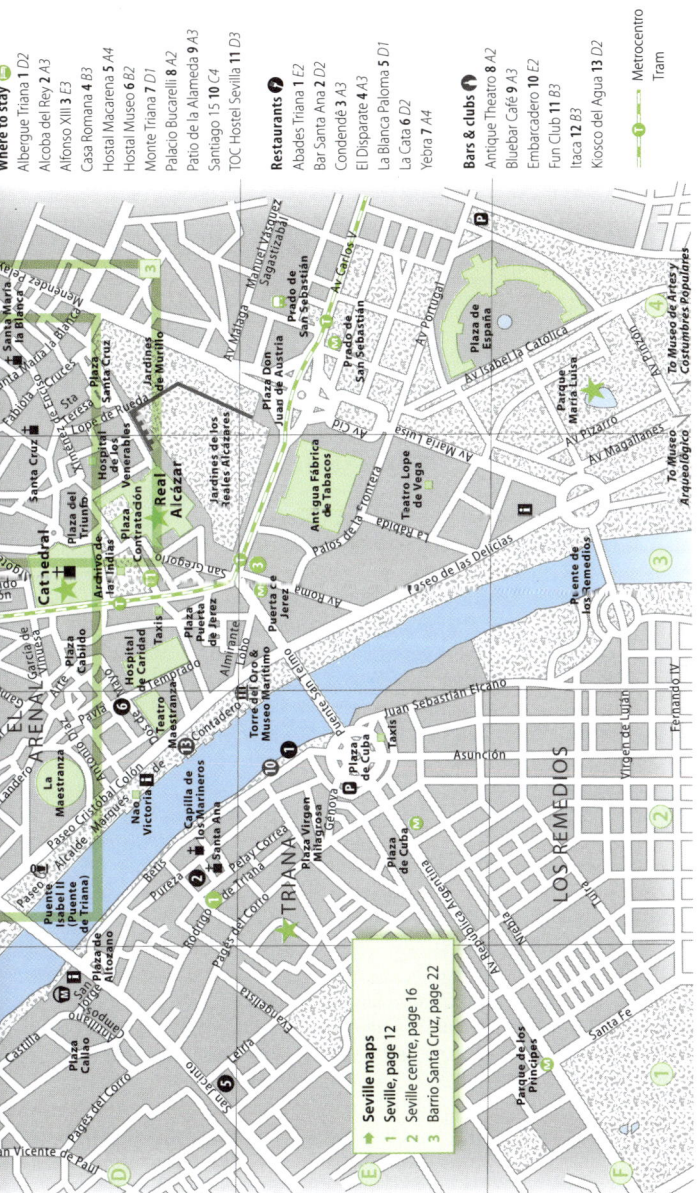

Seville maps
1 Seville, page 12
2 Seville centre, page 16
3 Barrio Santa Cruz, page 22

forget to look up once in a while to appreciate the lofty Gothic grandeur and the excellent stained glass, much of it by Heinrich of Germany (15th century) and Arnao of Flanders (16th century). At the western end of the church, Murillo's *Guardian Angel* stands to the left of the middle door, leading the Christ child by the hand.

Start on the north side, at the chapel of **San Antonio**, with a huge and much-admired Murillo of that saint's vision of a cloud of cherubs and angels. Above it is a smaller Baptism by the same artist. An impressive Renaissance baptismal font here is still in use, while a 15th-century frieze of saints adorns the *reja*. These *rejas* are works of art in their own right – some of them take wrought iron to extraordinary delicacy.

Arriving in the northeast corner, take a break from chapels and climb the **Giralda**. You reach the top via 35 ramps (if they weren't numbered you'd think you were in a never-ending Escher sketch), designed to allow sentries and muezzins to climb the tower on horseback. The tower is 94 m high and the view from the top is excellent and helps to orientate yourself in this confusing city. There's a host of bells up here; the oldest date from the 14th century. Note that the Giralda closes an hour earlier than the cathedral.

Coming down, the next chapel of **San Pedro** contains a *retablo* with nine good Zurbaráns devoted to the first pope's life. The inspiring **Royal Chapel** is often curtained off for services. The cuissons of its masterly domed ceiling contain busts of Castilla's kings and queens. In a funerary urn are the remains of the sainted conqueror-king Fernando III, while his wife Beatrice of Swabia (the inspiration behind Burgos cathedral) and their son Alfonso X (the Wise) are also buried here.

In the southeast corner, the treasury is entered through the **Mariscal Chapel**, which has a stunning altarpiece centred on the Purification of Mary and painted by Pedro de Campaña (Pieter Kempeneer), a Fleming of exalted talent. The **Treasury** contains a display of monstrances (one of which is said to hold a spine from the Crown of Thorns), salvers and processional crowns. A fine antechamber and courtyard adjoin the Chapter-house, adorned with vault paintings by Murillo.

The massive Main Sacristy is almost a church in its own right, with an ornate Plateresque entrance and three altars featuring fine paintings; a moving Descent from the Cross by Pedro de Campaña, a Santa Teresa by Zurbarán and a San Lorenzo by Jordán. Two Murillos face each other across the room; they depict two of the city's earliest archbishops from the Visigothic period, San Isidoro and San Leandro.

Columbus' tomb stands proud in the southern central doorway, borne aloft by four figures representing the kingdoms of Castilla, León, Aragón and Navarra. It's in late 19th-century Romantic style, and some remains were deposited here in 1902, which DNA testing has proved to be those of Columbus – Seville is one of four cities that claim to have part of his remains. Columbus spent time praying in the next chapel, which features an excellent 14th-century fresco of Mary, in the place where the mosque's *mihrab* once stood. The later *retablo* (altarpiece) was built around the painting.

The cathedral's principal devotional spaces are in the centre of the massive five-naved structure – the choir and the chancel. The choir itself is closed off by a noteworthy gilt Plateresque *reja* depicting the Tree of Jesse, while the ornate stalls feature misericords with charismatic depictions of demons and the vices.

The main *retablo* is a marvel of Christian art and is the largest altarpiece in the world. Measuring a gigantic 18 m by 28 m, it was masterminded by the Fleming Pieter Dancart, who began it in 1481; several other notable painters and sculptors worked on it until its completion in 1526. It is surmounted by a gilt canopy, atop which is a Calvary scene, and figures of the Apostles. The central panels depict the Ascension, Resurrection, Assumption and Nativity, while the other panels depict scenes from the life of Jesus and parts of the Old Testament.

You exit the church under the curious wooden crocodile known as El Lagarto (the lizard), probably a replica of a gift from an Egyptian ruler wooing a Spanish *infanta*. The pretty **Patio de los Naranjos** is another Moorish original, formerly the ablutions courtyard of the mosque. It's shaded with the orange trees that give it its name, as well as an irrigation system likely to trip you as your eyes adjust from the dusky interior. Admire the lofty Puerta de la Concepción (20th century, but faithful to the cathedral's style) before you exit through the Puerta del Perdón.

★ Real Alcázar

Plaza del Triunfo s/n, T954-502323, alcazarsevilla.org. Oct-Mar 0930-1700, Apr-Sep 0930-1900. €13.50. The informative free audio tour is downloaded from a QR code. Your ticket also includes entry to Antiquarium, Centro Ceramica Triana and Casa Fabiola.

Even if the delights of tapas and the heat of the day are seducing your hours in Seville away from you, don't head for home without seeing the Alcázar, as you'll be derided by any friends who have. While you'll see horseshoe arches, stucco, calligraphy and coffered ceilings throughout, it's not a Moorish palace. It used to be, but little remains from that period; it owes its Moorish look to the Castillian kings who built it after the Reconquest: Alfonso X and his enlightened son Pedro I.

As well as being a magnificent palace, the Alcázar was once a considerable fortress in this impressively fortified city, a fact easily appreciable as you pass through the chunky walls in the dramatic red Puerta del León entrance gate, named for the tiled king of beasts guarding it. You emerge on to a large courtyard dominated by the impressive façade of the main palace of the Castillian kings. Before heading into this, investigate the Patio del Yeso to the left, one of the few remaining Moorish structures, where lobed arches face horseshoe ones across a pool surrounded by myrtle hedges.

Opposite, across the courtyard, are chambers built by Fernando and Isabel to control New World affairs. Magellan planned his trip here, and there's an important *retablo* from this period of the Virgen de los Navegantes. In the main panel by Alejo Fernández, the Virgin spreads her protective mantle over Columbus, Carlos V and a shadowy group of indigenous figures (who might see some trouble coming if they could glimpse the side panel of Santiago, Spain's patron, who is gleefully decapitating Moors).

From this main courtyard, you access tours of the **upper floor (Cuarto Alto) of the palace**, still sometimes used when Spanish royals are in town. A series of elaborately furnished chambers are visited on the **guided tour** ⓘ *€5, prebook online*, which leaves half-hourly.

Museo de
Bellas Artes

Plaza
Museo

(A) Avenida
5 Cines

Taxis

Plaza del
Duque

San Vicente
Abad Gordillo
Jesús de la Vera Cruz
Santa Vicenta María

Alfonso XII

Monsalves

San Eloy

Fernán Caballero

Sauceda

Fray Diego de Deza

Pedro del Toro

San Roque

O'Donnell

Gravina

Pedro Mártir

Rafael González Abreu

Canalejas

Bailén

Murillo

José de Velilla

Plaza de la
Magdalena

Rioja

Velázquez

Muñoz Olivé

San

Ros

Tove

La Magdalena

Cristo Esteban

(B) Luis de Vargas

Marqués de Paradas

Gravina

San Pablo

Mateos

Plaza
Godinez

Moratín

Alemán

Méndez Núñez

Julio César

Sánchez Barcaíztegui

Zaragoza

Carlos Cañal

Bilbao

Tetuán

Plaza
Nueva

Ayuntam

Albuera

Trastámara

Reyes Católicos

Almansa

Taxis

(C) Taxis

9

Padre Marchena

Joaquín Guicho

Santas Patronas

Galera

Pastor y Landero

Castelar

Gamazo

6

Genil

Arenal

Adriano

Puente Isabel II
(Puente de Triana)

Paseo Cristóbal Colón

García de Vin

7

12

Federico Sánchez Bed

Plaza
Cabildo

Río Guadalquivir

Paseo Alcalde Marqués

La Maestranza

1

Circo

Antonia Díaz

Varflora

Pavía

General Castaños

San Diego

Arfe

2

3

3

(D)

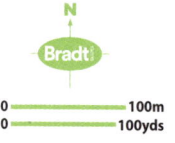

N

Bradt

0 ———— 100m
0 ———— 100yds

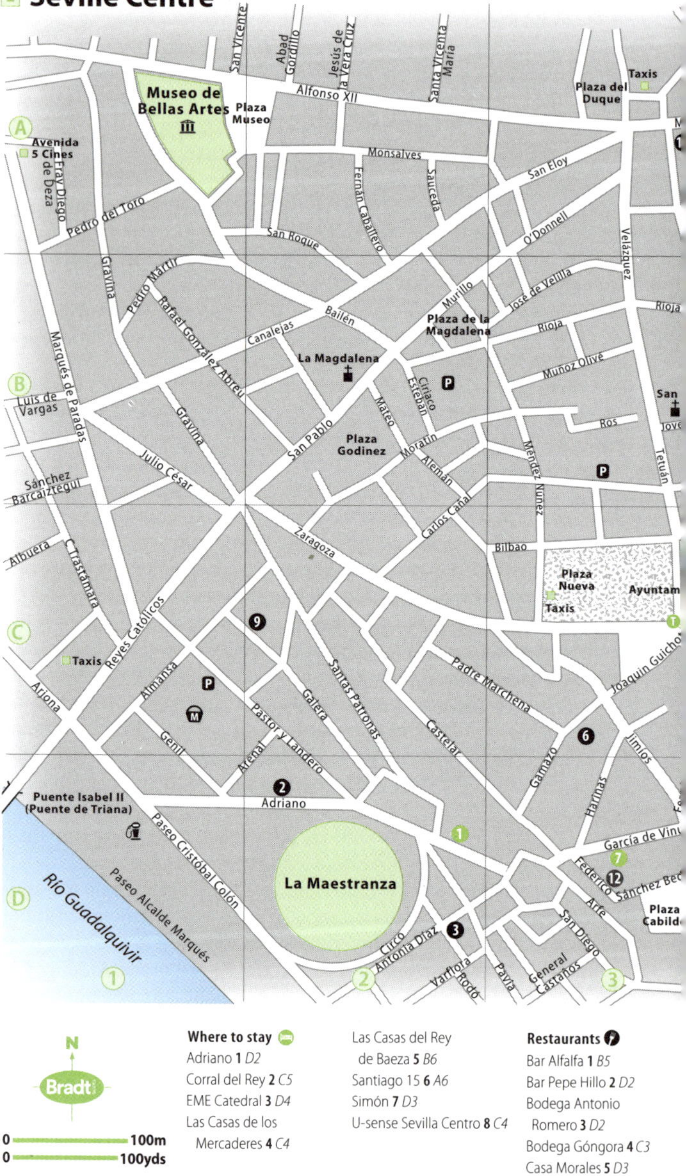

Where to stay 🛏
Adriano **1** *D2*
Corral del Rey **2** *C5*
EME Catedral **3** *D4*
Las Casas de los
  Mercaderes **4** *C4*

Las Casas del Rey
  de Baeza **5** *B6*
Santiago 15 **6** *A6*
Simón **7** *D3*
U-sense Sevilla Centro **8** *C4*

Restaurants 🍴
Bar Alfalfa **1** *B5*
Bar Pepe Hillo **2** *D2*
Bodega Antonio
  Romero **3** *D2*
Bodega Góngora **4** *C3*
Casa Morales **5** *D3*

Casa Moreno **6** *C3*
El Rinconcillo **7** *A6*
La Antigua
  Bodeguita **8** *B4*
La Brunilda **9** *C2*
La Campana **10** *A3*
Taberna Zurbarán **11** *A4*

Bars & clubs
Groucho **12** *D3*

Metrocentro
Tram

Semana Santa

Seville's Holy Week processions are an unforgettable sight. Mesmeric candlelit lines of hooded figures and cross-carrying penitents make their way through the streets accompanied by the mournful notes of a brass band and two large *pasos*, one with a scene from the Passion, one with a statue of Mary. These scenes aren't unusual in Spain but what makes it so special is the *sevillanos'* extraordinary respect and interest for the event and devotion to the sculptures.

The Semana Santa processions originated in medieval times, becoming firmly established in the 16th century. The brotherhoods wanted to demonstrate their faith with a display of penitence, while the eerily lifelike wooden effigies by master sculptors were designed to engage the public and teach them about the final days of Christ's life, and his death and subsequent resurrection.

Today, members of 60 *cofradías* (brotherhoods) practise intensively for their big moment, when they leave their church and walk through the streets to the *carrera oficial*, a route leading along Calle Sierpes and through Plaza San Francisco to the cathedral, and then home again. Some brotherhoods have over 2000 in the procession, consisting of *nazarenos*, who wear pointed hoods, *penitentes*, who carry crosses, and *costaleros*, who carry the *pasos*. Each *paso* is accompanied by a band that plays haunting brass laments and deep thuds of drums.

Brotherhoods go out from Palm Sunday until Easter Sunday, but the most important processions are on the night of Maundy Thursday (*la madrugá*), when several brotherhoods go to the cathedral during the wee hours.

Sevillanos hold the processions in great esteem and a high percentage are members of a *cofradía*, even if they're not really religious. Everyone has their favourite sculpture too; the best-loved Marys are La Macarena and La Esperanza de Triana. The most admired Christs are El Cachorro and Jesús del Gran Poder, both supreme pieces of art. During the processions, it's not uncommon for people on the street or on balconies to launch into a *saeta*, a haunting flamenco-based song inspired by the *paso*; similarly, the Marys are often greeted with shouts of '*Guapa!*'.

What to take

Pick up a printed programme of the processions (listing the route, timings, tunic colour and statues of each procession) from hotels, shops and tourist offices; alternatively download a PDF from *Diario de Sevilla* or *ABC*, or use an app such as El Penitente. Make sure you're dosed up with suncream if it's a hot day, but don't bother with an umbrella; the *cofradías* stay home if it's wet, because the rain damages the *pasos*.

What to see

If you're in Seville for the week, you'll see plenty of processions. Just pick a few each day, and then go at it hard on the Thursday night. The busiest places are near the *cofradía*'s own church and the cathedral (be aware that the *carrera oficial*, the last stretch into the cathedral, is seating only). There are fewer people on the *cofradía*'s return journey.

Your best bet for a good view, if you'd prefer to avoid the crowded streets (good-natured, but fairly intense) is to either book a hotel or apartment near one of the churches (all accommodation is pricey during this period), or to book a balcony, often with snacks and drinks provided (book online at balcones-semana-santa-sevilla.com). You can always pop downstairs and venture into the streets to take in the charged atmosphere, then nip back up to enjoy your vantage point. Some of the most interesting are:

La Paz (Palm Sunday) The first *cofradía* and the only one to pass through María Luisa park. Watch it with the spectacular backdrop of Plaza de España at around 1430-1530.

San Esteban (Tuesday) Their exit (1730-1830) and entry (0030-0130) from a church just behind the Casa de Pilatos is great to watch as the manoeuvring of the *pasos* is a difficult feat. Get there a long time before.

Las Siete Palabras (Wednesday) This 16th-century *cofradía* has an excellent Calvary as one of their *pasos*. Be in Plaza Gavidia from 2030.

La Madrugá Late on Thursday night, six of the most important *cofradías* make the journey. It's worth making the effort to stay up all night, as most of the city does. First up is El Silencio, a 14th-century brotherhood and one of the oldest. Although it's not completely silent, its black-robed *nazarenos* are an eerie sight. See it from Plaza del Duque from 0100 and stay there for Jesús del Gran Poder, whose stunning Christ follows hard on their heels. Then trot north to the Alameda de Hércules, for the procession of La Macarena. At about 0230, try to be at the Puente de Triana to watch her great rival La Esperanza de Triana cross the river. If you're still on two feet, head to Plaza Encarnación to see Los Gitanos, the well-loved gypsy *cofradía*.

El Cachorro/La O (Friday) Both these Triana *cofradías* cross the Puente de San Telmo and the Puente de Triana on their way home at 2330-0030.

La Resurrección (Sunday) Leaving their Macarena home at 0830, they reach the cathedral about 1130, where there's enough room to see them, the last of the processions.

Etiquette
Be silent when watching the *pasos* pass, and don't applaud unless other people are so doing. It is considered rude to cross a procession; definitely don't do it in front of the *paso* or among the band.

Timing
If you've got to be somewhere at a certain time during Semana Santa, allow plenty of it, as you're likely to get caught in crowds watching a procession.

What to eat
Semana Santa is all about the sweet, sticky pastries: *torrijas* – bread slices soaked in egg, milk, sugar and cinnamon and then fried and drizzled with honey; and *pestiños* – fried dough with honey, sesame seeds and aniseed.

BACKGROUND

Seville

While Seville legend attributes the founding of the city to Hercules, it is likely that the first permanent settlements on this site were built by the Tartessians in the first half of the first millennium BC.

The Phoenicians established themselves here shortly afterwards, and they extended and fortified the existing town. It became an important trading centre in the Western Mediterranean, and continued to be so after a Carthaginian takeover in the third century BC. In 206 BC, the Romans defeated them in the battle of Ilipa, near the city that they named Hispalis. They also established the town of Itálica nearby, originally as a rest camp for mutinous Italian soldiers. The river in these days was known as the Baetis. Caesar arrived here as administrator of the town and enjoyed his stay by all accounts. The people sided with him against his arch-rival Pompey and in 45 BC were rewarded by being conferred full Roman citizenship. When Augustus created the province of Baetica, Hispalis soon became the capital, and both it and Itálica became very important Roman cities. The emperor Trajan was born in the latter and Hadrian grew up there. Christianity took early root in Seville and, after early persecutions, soon flourished.

The city was sacked by Vandals and Swabians as the Empire collapsed, but then prospered under Visigothic rule, with the wise historian and archbishop San Isidoro particularly prominent. The Islamic invasion in 711 put an end to the Visigothic kingdom; Hispalis was transliterated to Isbiliyya, from which Seville is derived, and the river was renamed *al wadi al kibir* (big river), or Guadalquivir as it is now written. Seville spent the first few centuries of the Moorish occupation under the shadow of Córdoba, but, on the collapse of the caliphate in 1031, became an independent *taifa* state and grew rapidly to be the most powerful one in Al-Andalus. Under the poet-king Al-Mu'tamid, the city experienced an exceptional flourishing of wealth and culture. Much of Seville's Moorish architectural heritage dates from the 12th century and the Almohad regime.

In 1248, Isbiliyya was conquered by Fernando III, and initially much of its

The palace façade is a fusion of Christian and Moorish styles that just about achieves harmony. Inscriptions about the glory of Allah (Pedro had a deep interest in Islamic culture) adjoin more conventional Spanish ones proclaiming royal greatness.

This fusion is repeated throughout this whole section, centred around the stunning **Patio de las Doncellas**. Throughout the complex are *azulejos*, topped by friezes of ceramic decoration, while higher up, intricate stucco friezes are surmounted by a range of marvellous inlaid ceilings. Also worth admiring are the imposing doors, some elaborately inlaid. Among the rooms off this courtyard are the **Salón de Embajadores**, with a beautiful half-orange ceiling and a frieze of Spanish kings; and the chapel, where Carlos V married his first cousin Isabella of

Muslim population were expelled and their lands divided among noble families. Later Pedro I, great-grandson of Fernando III, oversaw largely tolerant Judeo-Islamic multiculturalism. However, in 1391, a massive anti-Jewish pogrom saw synagogues forcibly changed into churches and the Jewish quarter, one of Iberia's largest, virtually ceased to exist. The current cathedral was begun soon afterwards.

With the discovery of the New World, Seville's Golden Age began. In 1503, it was granted a monopoly on trade with the transatlantic colonies, and became one of the largest and most prosperous cities in Europe.

The 17th century was the zenith of Seville's school of painting, with artists such as Zurbarán, Murillo and Velázquez all operating. However, the expulsion of the *moriscos* (converted Moors) in 1610 hit the city hard and merchants left to ply their trade elsewhere. A plague in 1649 killed an incredible half of the inhabitants, and in 1717, with the Guadalquivir silting up rapidly, New World trade was moved to Cádiz.

Occupied by the French from 1810 to 1812, Seville only really rose from its torpor in the 20th century. The massive Ibero-American exhibition of 1929 bankrupted the city but created the infrastructure for a modern city and many fine public spaces. In the Civil War, the brutal General Queipo de Llano bluffed his way into control of the city. Workers from Triana and Macarena struggled against the rising and were mercilessly repressed, and the 36-year dictatorship was a period of extreme hardship.

In 1982, the Sevillano Felipe González was elected the first Socialist prime minister since the Civil War, governing until 1996. The city, beginning to stir once more, hosted a World Cup semifinal and, 10 years later, Expo 1992, having already become the capital of autonomous Andalucía. The event left the city with enormous debts but attracted some 18 million visitors and boosted Seville's international profile.

The city continues with urban improvements, with the metro and tram system up and running, and extensive pedestrianisation of the old centre implemented. Unemployment, poverty and homelessness are still massive, if not always visible, problems. For more, see 'History', page 63.

Portugal (one of many inbreedings that doomed the Habsburg line).

Adjacent is the **Gothic Palace**, heavily altered from the original by Carlos V and his descendants. From here stretches the vast and fantastic garden; different sections filled with slurping carp, strutting peacocks, palm trees and a grotesque gallery built into a section of the old walls – it's worth climbing up and walking along for the view either side. Steps lead down to the picturesque covered pool known as **Los Baños de Doña María de Padilla**. The garden has featured in several films and series, most famously in *Game of Thrones* (it was House Martell's Water Gardens of Dorne). You finally exit the complex through the vestibule where coaches and horses used to roll in, and you emerge in the Patio de Banderas. There are often small exhibitions upstairs in the vestibule.

Archivo de las Indias

Plaza del Triunfo s/n, T954-500528. Tue-Sat 0930-1630, Sun 1000-1330. 15 Jul-31 Aug Mon-Fri 0830-1430. Free.

This square and sober Renaissance building – 'An immense icebox of granite guarded by lions, in which is housed the colonial past, every sigh and every comma, until the end of the world' (C Nooteboom, *Roads to Santiago*) – between the cathedral and Alcázar was once Seville's Lonja, where merchants met to broker trade with the New World. Goods that came back from the Americas and East Indies included gold, silver, tobacco, sugar, spices and silk.

In the late 18th century it was converted into the state archive, where all 80 million documents relating to the Americas were stored and filed, an intriguing record that includes everything from the excited scribblings of Columbus to the

Where to stay 🛏
Amadeus & La Música **1** *B4*
Casa del Poeta **2** *B3*
El Rey Moro **3** *C3*
Goya **4** *B3*

Hotel and Suites Murillo **5** *C3*
Las Casas de
  la Judería **6** *B5*
Pensión
  San Pancracio **7** *B4*

Restaurants 🍴
Bodega Santa Cruz **1** *C*
Casa Román **2** *C3*
Cervecería Giralda **3** *B*
La Goleta **4** *B2*

0 ———— 50m
0 ———— 50yds

most mundane book-keeping of remote jungle outposts. There's a small display of the building's history on the ground floor, and upstairs, under the vaulted stone ceilings and among the polished shelves holding the archives, are regular themed exhibitions and a couple of Goya portraits. Look out for the bronze cannon fabricated in Seville, sunk on a ship near Cuba, located using Archive documents and returned to Spain in 1976.

Barrio Santa Cruz

Seville's most charming barrio: small plazas shaded by orange trees

Once home to much of Seville's Jewish population, atmospheric Barrio Santa Cruz has a web of narrow pedestrian lanes. Squeezed between the Alcázar, cathedral and a road tracing the old city walls, it's very touristy but thankfully not over-prettified, and there's a fairly standard tour that you can easily explore away from. There are excellent accommodation and restaurant options as well as several intriguing antique and handicraft shops.

The best way to enter the barrio is from the Plaza del Triunto by the cathedral, head through the gate in the Alcázar walls to the south into the pretty square of Patio de Banderas, floored with sand and lined with orange trees. In the opposite corner, duck through a small tunnel and twist and turn your way on to Calle Judería, one of the nooks with most medieval flavour.

A wander through the narrow lanes of Barrio Santa Cruz will reveal much. On one side, the area is bounded by the public park of the Jardines de Murillo, centred around a monument to Columbus, and with a well-frequented kids' playground, handily located but lacking shade. Nearby, at the bottom of Calle Santa María la Blanca, Puerta de la Carne (Meat Gate) was once one of the city's entrances; farmers would enter here with carts piled high with meats, cereals and vegetables. It's well worth visiting the small **church**, formerly

Seville maps
1 Seville, page 12
2 Seville centre, page 16
3 Barrio Santa Cruz, page 22

González de León

Verde

6

Archeros

Plaza Curtidores

anta María la Blanca

Caño y Cueto

Menéndez Pelayo

cellas

Puerta de la Carne

5

Paseo Catalina de Ribera

Paseo Catalina de Ribera

illo

To Prado San Sebastián Bus Station

5

6

a mosque and then a synagogue ⓘ *www.santamarialablanca.com, Sep-Jun Mon-Thu 1130-1300, 1800-1900*, that gives the street its name. The attractive toothed arch of the portal gives little hint of the Baroque fantasy inside – the central vault of the triple-naved church is carved with a riot of floral and vegetal decoration. In the left aisle you'll see a fine yet underrated Murillo, a *Last Supper*. A young, visionary Christ is surrounded by the wise, bearded old heads of his apostles. It's all the better for being in situ.

Hospital de los Venerables
Plaza de los Venerables 8.

In the heart of Barrio Santa Cruz, and built at the end of the 17th century in a charitable vein, the Venerables refers to the old priests for whom it was originally intended as a hospital and residence. While the hospital itself is currently closed for refurbishment until 2026/7, the church opens for organ recitals (see *catedraldesevilla.com*), and is worth visiting as a repository of fine paintings of the late Sevillian school. The church is set alongside the main courtyard, a noble space centred around a sunken fountain and surrounded by an arcade on marble columns. Stunning tile-work completes the effect.

Now managed by the archdiocese, the hospital will be used to display religious artworks from the Cathedral's collection. Meanwhile, after nearly 40 years here, the Focus-Abengoa foundation's collection of paintings by Velázquez, especially his early works, as well those as by Murillo and Zurbarán, is moving to Sala San Hermenegildo on Plaza Concordia, next to the main El Corte Inglés, opening in 2026.

Aire Ancient Baths
C Aire 15, T919-032214, www.beaire.com. Mon-Thu 1000-2200, Fri 1000-2400, Sat 0900-2400, Sun 0900-2200. Basic visit €65 for 90 minutes. Wide menu of massages and other treatments.

Located in a 16th-century palace, this luxurious Arabian-style bathhouse offers warm, hot and cold baths as well as an aromatherapy steam room, jet bath and salt-water bath, and deliciously indulgent treatments such as the Argan Foam Ritual. Massages over 45 minutes include a brief slot in the rooftop pool. The place itself is beautifully relaxing, with delicate lighting and stylish design. Only a certain number of people are allowed in at a time, so it pays to reserve a slot in advance by phone or via the website. Take a bathing suit; you can hire one if necessary.

Casa Fabiola Donación Mariano Bellver
C Fabiola 5, T955-470295, www.sevilla.org/actualidad/casa-fabiola. Tue-Sun 1100-1900. €3.

Opened in October 2018, Museo Bellver exhibits a superb collection of mostly 19th-century *Costumbrismo* – painting, sculpture, furniture and ceramics – put together by Don Mariano Bellver Utrera and his wife Dolores Mejías since the 1960s. There are also exhibitions and occasional performances.

Much of this area is taken up with the large Parque María Luisa, donated to the city by Queen Isabel II's sister in the late 19th century. It was used as the site for the grandiose 1929 Ibero-American Exhibition, an event on a massive scale that the Primo de Rivera dictatorship hoped would re-establish Seville and Spain in the world spotlight. The legacy of the exhibition is a much-loved public park, the monumental Plaza de España, and a beautiful series of the former pavilions. On Calle San Fernando, the massive and elegant Hotel Alfonso XIII was built to accommodate important visitors to the exhibition.

Antigua Fábrica de Tabacos
C San Fernando 4, T954-551000. Mon-Fri 0800-2100, Sat 0800-1400, Sun closed. Free.

Next door to the Alfonso XIII hotel stands what was once Spain's second-largest building, surrounded by a fence and moat. This was originally the tobacco factory, complete with its own chapel and prison, and workers were carefully checked to make sure they didn't steal any cigarettes. Visitors flocked to the factory in the late 19th century to see the girls at work, some of whom were gypsies from Triana, for it had been made famous by *Carmen* and other tales of the beauty of Seville's womenfolk. The numerous elegant hallways and courtyards suit its new function perfectly as a university building. It's a lively place and worth a visit to wander around its corridors.

★ Parque María Luisa
Daily 0800-2400 summer (2200 winter). Free.

This beautiful and peaceful space is Seville's best park, again developed for the 1929 exhibition. It's full of quiet corners, even on busy days, and a series of informative plaques detail the huge range of exotic trees and plants on show.

Around the park are dotted various buildings erected for the 1929 exhibition. The most grandiose of these is the Plaza de España, envisaged as a second Giralda, a symbol of a new, dynamic Seville. The semicircular area is backed by a massive brick and marble building that curves around to two proud towers. A small canal used for leisurely rowing is crossed by four bridges. The most endearing feature is the series of alcoves dedicated to Spain's provinces. A tiled map of each is accompanied by the depiction of a significant historical event. The buildings are used now for various government departments, but it's no surprise that the stunning ensemble has been used in several films, featuring as part of Cairo in *Lawrence of Arabia* and Naboo in *Star Wars: The Attack of the Clones*, and Wadiya in *The Dictator*.

At the other end of the park are two excellent museums. The **Museo de Artes y Costumbres Populares** ⓘ *Plaza de América 3, T955-542951, Jul-Aug Tue-Sun 0900-1500, Sep-Jun Tue-Sat 0900-2100, Sun 0900-1500, free for EU citizens, €1.50*

Feria de Abril

Seville's April fiesta is a lively counterpoint to the solemnity of the Semana Santa processions. Originally a gypsy horse fair, it took its present form in the early 20th century. It gets bigger and livelier every year, with the well-loved Los Remedios grounds being squeezed to the limit by well over 1000 *casetas*.

The *casetas* are colourfully striped tents, venues for six days of socialising, eating, drinking *manzanilla* and dancing *sevillanas*. Most are privately owned by social clubs, employers or families; bar a few public ones, entry is by invitation only. It's busy day and night; during the afternoon *sevillanos* dashingly dressed in riding suits and bright *flamenca* costumes parade by on horseback and in elegant carriages, while the dancing and drinking action hots up at night. A large funfair adds to the attraction as do the season's biggest bullfights, held at the Maestranza.

Getting there The massive Feria gate is at the bottom of Calle Asunción, a 15-minute walk from the Puente de San Telmo and nearby Plaza de Cuba metro station. Shuttle buses run from Prado San Sebastián. Cars are not allowed near the grounds. Taxis are, but you're much better walking home as the queues are horrendous. Or order an Uber from the back exit (Puente de la Delicias) rather than by the front gate.

Kick-off The Feria begins on the Monday night two weeks and a day after Easter Sunday. Crowds wait until midnight, when the gate (*portada*; a new one is built each year) is spectacularly lit up and the party begins. The Feria runs until the next Sunday, when a fireworks display east of the gate officially ends the revelry at midnight.

Casetas Grab a map from tourist information or download a PDF on your phone. Most of the public *casetas* are clearly marked; these belong to political parties and the neighbourhood councils of the city. If you know a local that

others, is in the rather majestic *mudéjar* pavilion. On the ground floor, you can see temporary exhibitions, and, on the veranda, information about the pavilion, its architect Aníbal González and Seville's two Expos (1929, directed by the visionary González, and 1992).

The basement presents a fascinating walk through multitudinous aspects of Andalucian life from the mundane – food prep, domestic hygiene and heating – to an outstanding celebration of artisan skills: from cork harvesting to lacemaking, esparto grass-weaving and castanet-making, precious metals and ironwork. In addition, you can see different types of *azulejos* (glazed ceramic tiles), plus pottery lamps and *lebrillos* (large bowls). La Cartuja chinaware (see page 36), teetering on the edge of collapse after almost 200 years, has its own small section.

Seville's **Museo Arqueológico** ⓘ *Pabellón de Bellas Artes, Plaza de América s/n, T954-120632* should be good, considering the wealth of peoples that have lived and traded in the region since prehistoric times. This mighty museum, housed in can invite you in to a *caseta*, well and good, but you could try to get into some of the less exclusive ones, especially those located further from the *portada*, and preferably later in the week.

Dress respectably and ask the doorman politely in Spanish if you can enter; you'll get plenty of knockbacks but also plenty of entries, particularly (doormen being doormen) if a woman does the asking and is wearing a dress, flower and shawl. Large groups of people speaking English will likely get in nowhere, especially if not dressed smartly. Shorts and a T-shirt won't cut it; men should wear long trousers and a button-down shirt, and women a dress or stylish outfit. Up until about 2100, and especially from Thursday, some *casetas* don't have doormen.

Eating and drinking The *casetas* put on a range of tapas and *raciones*, although usually at inflated prices. Drink *manzanilla* (usually served in a half-bottle) or *rebujito*, a weaker refreshing blend of the same with lemonade, served in a litre jug. *Pescaíto frito* (fried fish) is traditionally eaten on the first night of Feria; other popular sharing dishes served throughout the six days include cheese, *jamón ibérico*, *tortilla*, prawns and croquettes. In all the *casetas*, once the eating's done, people spend most of the night dancing. The *sevillana* is a relatively modern form with roots in both flamenco and Latin music. A dance has four distinct parts, all characterised by elaborate arms-aloft movements, partners stepping around each other, and stares of moody intensity. You'll experience another dimension of Feria if you manage to learn the basics.

Kicking on Unless you've hit a manic *caseta*, Feria winds down about 0300. If you want more, the best places are around the Feria grounds on and near Calle Asunción. The biggest night at Feria is usually the Tuesday, because Wednesday is a holiday in Seville. The weekend has a different vibe – locals head to the beach, and out-of-towners flood in.

Toilets Be warned that queues in all *casetas* are long; you may have to wait 20 minutes. Bring tissues as rolls of paper soon run out.

the vast Expo 1929 Fine Arts, or Renaissance, Pavilion, also designed by Aníbal González, was closed at the time of updating. A €28 million refurbishment is being carried out by architect Guillermo Vázquez Consuegra; closed since 2023, the museum is scheduled to reopen in 2027. Limited information has been provided about the museum's new incarnation, other than that it will feature more interactive exhibits. Many of the current pieces are likely to remain, including a particularly rich Roman collection. From the prehistoric period, pieces from the Tartessian culture (people who lived in the Guadalquivir valley from about 1100 BC onwards) are outstanding. The star attraction from this era is the Carambolo treasure: 21 pieces of finely worked gold jewellery – necklaces, bracelets and plaques – showing Phoenician influence. The hoard was found by chance in nearby Camas in 1958. Iberian stone lions are also impressive, and look out for *idolos*, small anthropomorphic figures or 'plates' (flat pieces) dating from the Copper Age; most were discovered in the many dolmens nearby.

The Roman finds, mostly from nearby Itálica and Carmona, include a second-century AD headless Venus, a Diana, the emperor Trajan in full heroic mode, and a bearded Hadrian. A mosaic from Écija depicts the Triumph of Bacchus, his chariot drawn by leashed leopards. More recent finds include 19 amphorae filled with bronze Roman coins found in a park near Seville.

★ Triana

backstreet flamenco bars, riverside restaurants and colourful tiles

Many visitors find that Triana becomes their favourite part of Seville. It's redolent with history from every epoch of the Christian city as well as having a picturesque riverfront lined with terraced bars and restaurants. It was for a long time the gypsy barrio and as such the home of flamenco in Seville. Although most of the gypsies were moved on in the 1950s, its backstreet bars are still the best place to catch impromptu performances. Triana is also famous for ceramics; most of the *azulejo* tiles that decorate Seville's houses so beautifully come from here, and there are still some workshops in the area. It's also got a significant maritime history.

Entering the barrio across the Puente Isabel II, you arrive at Plaza de Altozano. From here, Calle Betis stretches to your left along the riverfront and is one of the top strolls in the city, lined with prettily coloured buildings, most of which are dedicated to eating and drinking.

Behind here, on Calle Pureza, is the **Iglesia de Santa Ana** ⓘ *Vázquez de Leca 1, Sep-Jun Mon-Fri 1030-1900, Jul-Aug Mon-Fri 1030-1400, €4.* The 'Cathedral of Triana' is believed to be Seville's oldest church, dating from around 1276.

Not far from here, at Calle Pureza 53, La Esperanza de Triana lives in an ornate *retablo* behind the big yellow-and-white façade of the **Capilla de los Marineros** ⓘ *Mon-Sat 1000-1330, 1800-2130, Sun 1000-1400, 1800-2030, free.* She and La Macarena are the two most-adored Virgins of the city, and there are few bars around without a picture up of one or the other of them. Her passages across the bridges in the wee hours of Good Friday morning are among the most emotional of the Semana Santa processions; see box, page 18.

On the other side of Triana, the **Capilla de Patrocinio** ⓘ *C Castilla 182, May-Sep Tue-Sat 1100-1300, 1915-2115, Sun 1100-1300, Oct-Apr Tue-Sat 1100-1300, 1815-2015, Sun 1100-1300, free,* is worth a visit for the superb Christ inside, who is much revered across Seville. He is named El Cachorro, after a dead young gypsy that the sculptor is said to have used as a model. The sculpture is breathtaking; you can feel the sinews of the crucified Christ straining, while his face is a perfectly rendered mixture of anguish and relief.

If you look at a picture of Seville in the early 19th century or before, you'll see that, from the Moorish Torre del Oro, the city wall recedes from the riverbank, leaving a large open area, El Arenal (meaning sandy spot). This was a haunt of thieves, swindlers, prostitutes and smugglers, who hung out near the docks where the action was. It was built over in the 19th century, and El Arenal is now one of Seville's most pleasant barrios, with some of the city's major landmarks.

Torre del Oro
Paseo de Colón, T954-222419. Mon-Fri 0930-1845, Sat-Sun 1030-1845. €3, free Mon.

The spiky battlements of this beautiful Moorish tower are one of Seville's primary landmarks and the building is powerfully evocative of the city's military and maritime history. According to one theory, the exterior was once decorated with bright golden ceramic tiles, from which it gets its name. The interior now holds a motley maritime museum with sharks' teeth and paintings of galleons and salty sea-dogs, as well as plenty of model ships, that aren't illuminated by any explanatory panels. It's worth going in, however, for the great river views from the top, for the nicely presented timeline of the tower's history, and for the old prints showing Seville in the late 16th century. Triana has its boat-bridge and castle, and the docks are bristling with ships.

Nao Victoria
Paseo Alcalde Marqués de Contadero. T954-470891, www.fundacionnaovictoria.org. Daily Jan-Feb, Nov-Dec 1000-1800, Mar-Jun, Sep-Oct 1000-2000, Jul-Aug 0930-1430. €10

Lone survivor of Ferdinand Magellan's foolhardy expedition to the Spice Islands, *Nao Victoria* was the first ship to circumnavigate the world, in 1519-1522. *Nao Victoria 500* is a floating, living history lesson: having sailed 48,000 nautical miles, the full-scale replica is now permanently moored in the old port. Climb aboard to get a feel for the endless cramped weeks at sea subsisting on ship's biscuit and rank water. The small visitor centre on dry land sets the context for the extraordinary voyage – why it went, who was on it, what they ate, and how they navigated the oceans.

La Real Maestranza de Caballería – the Bullring
Paseo de Colón 12, T954-224577, www.realmaestranza.com. Daily Oct-Mar 0930-1900, Apr-Sep 0930-2100, except bullfight days, Palm Sunday and Feria week 0930-1500, otherwise May, Jun & Sep 0930-1900. €12.

One of Spain's principal temples of bullfighting, La Maestranza (not to be confused with the nearby theatre of the same name) is a beautiful building wedged into a city block, which accounts for its slightly elliptical shape. Started in the mid-18th century, it took until the late 1800s to finish it. The bullring holds some 12,000 spectators, and sells out nearly every seat during the April Feria, when the most prestigious fights of the season are held. The Seville crowd are among the most knowledgeable of aficionados, and many of bullfighting's most famous names have been *sevillanos*. The main entrance, La Puerta del Príncipe, has an imposing wrought-iron gateway by Pedro Roldán; it's a 16th-century work that originally stood in a convent. If a *torero* has a particularly good day, he is carried out through this door. The visit, guided by a QR-accessed audio tour, takes you first to a gallery of bullfighting-themed art in the former infirmary – paintings, ceramics and fans showing the various stages of the corrida, including a set of 12 Goyas. Next you learn about the sport's military origins, see the vividly coloured, gold-embroidered *trajes de luces* (bullfighters' suits), and meet famous figures such as Pepe Hillo and Curro Romero, whose statue stands outside. After the stables and the tiny chapel, you set foot on to the hallowed *albero* (ochre-coloured sand), source of Seville's ubiquitous yellow shade.

Hospital de Caridad
C Temprado 3.

Behind the theatre is this *residencia de ancianos* (nursing home) still fulfilling its original charitable purpose. Note that the hospital – both the main building and the chapel – is closed to visitors for refurbishment until late 2026. It was built as a hospital for the poor by Miguel de Mañara, a curious 17th-century *sevillano* often likened to Don Juan. After a scandalous youth of seduction and deceit he reformed completely when he saw a vision of his own death and dedicated himself to a life of charity and religion. He had a good eye for art; as a result of this, the hospital chapel has a collection of masterpieces commissioned by Mañara expressly to remind his brotherhood of the charitable virtues and the ultimate futility of worldly wealth and pride.

Two astonishing paintings stand above and opposite the entrance. They are the two finest, and most disturbing, works of the Sevillian painter Juan de Valdés Leal. The first one you'll see depicts a leering skeletal Death with a scythe, putting out a candle with one hand while trampling over objects that represent worldly wealth, power and knowledge. The inscription *In Ictu Oculi* translates as 'In the blink of an eye'. Opposite this is an even more challenging painting entitled *Finis Gloriae Mundi* ('The end of worldly glory'). It depicts a crypt in which a dead bishop and knight are being eaten by worms. Above, a balance scale is borne by the hand of Christ. On one side are symbols of the seven deadly sins, on the other side symbols of a holy love between God and Christ. 'Neither more nor less', read the words on the scales. Mañara commissioned these works in detail, and the face of the knight is thought to be his own.

After these grim warnings, the paintings of Murillo demonstrate the charitable life Mañara wanted his brotherhood to lead. Although four are missing (they were stolen by Napoleon's pillaging general, Soult, and are now scattered around the world; they include the impressive *Return of the Prodigal Son* in Washington), those that remain are exceptional examples of this artist's work. St John of God carries a sick man, while St Isabelle of Hungary cares for the afflicted. A Moses horned with light brings forth water from the rock, while Jesus feeds the multitude with loaves and fishes. In a *retablo* by Bernardo Simón de Pineda next to the pulpit is another Murillo painting, a depiction of the Annunciation. The sculptor Pedro Roldán is responsible for the figures in the intense *retablo* of Santo Cristo de la Caridad, with a Christ dripping blood flanked by cherubs. The main *retablo*, a Churrigueresque riot of cherubs and *salomónica* columns, is again the work of Roldán and Pineda; the former responsible for the emotive central tableau of the burial of Christ.

Juan de Valdés Leal painted the ceiling, of which the cupola is particularly fine, while Murillo also painted the small panels of the infants Jesus and John the Baptist above two other *retablos*.

Centro and San Vicente

Seville's shopping heartland

The busy Centro region is centred on the shopping streets of Sierpes, Tetuán, Velázquez, Cuna and O'Donnell. It's a fascinating stroll around this area, with the inevitable number of high-street fashion stores, as well as traditional shops selling sevillano Feria essentials such as *trajes de flamenca* (dresses), shoes, jewellery, fans and shawls. For independent boutiques, head for calles Don Alonso el Sabio and Pérez Galdós in Alfalfa.

★ El Ayuntamiento
Plaza Nueva 1, T955-010010. www.sevilla.org, check online for visiting details.

It's hard to miss Seville's town hall as it fronts two major squares, Plaza Nueva and Plaza San Francisco. It was formerly the site of one of Seville's most important monasteries; in the disentailment of 1835, this was demolished and the hitherto small Ayuntamiento expanded. As such, the building has two distinct sections: a Plateresque and a neoclassical (as well as some more recent annexes). From Plaza San Francisco, you can admire the superbly intricate stonework of the original 16th-century building. The architect of the newer structure thought he'd better continue with the Plateresque design to ensure harmony, but was stopped in his tracks by outraged neoclassicists appalled at the perceived flippancy; the Plateresque stonework thus comes to an abrupt and jagged end.

The interior, entered through the sober façade on Plaza Nueva, is a revelation. Before the Covid pandemic, guided tours were offered (Spanish only, but worth doing whatever your linguistic ability) – it is hoped that these will start up again in 2026. The visits take in the chambers of the original edifice, with breathtaking Renaissance stonework that still features Gothic influences. The lower council chamber is entered through a dignified doorway crowned with a depiction of Fernando III; inside there's an amazing coffered stone ceiling with busts of 36 monarchs in the coffers, finishing with Carlos V himself in one corner, complete with imperial crown. There are several elegant rooms on the top floor; notable works of art up here include a Zurbarán *Inmaculada* and a sketch by Murillo.

Setas de Sevilla

Plaza de la Encarnación, www.setasdesevilla.com. Viewing platform daily 0930-0030. €16 including two visits within 48 hours, audio guide via app and a short film about Seville. Museum Tue-Sat 1000-1930, Sun 1000-1330, €2.10.

This striking and controversial structure in central Seville has a viewing platform that is a magical place to be at sunset. Consisting of six giant interlinked parasol-like structures – Las Setas (the mushrooms) – it was designed by H Jürgen Mayer. The ground floor holds the traditional food market and, in the basement, is an archaeological museum based around the Roman and Moorish remains discovered below street level. From here, take the lift to a spectacular series of walkways 27 metres up among the city's rooftops, giving great views in all directions.

★Casa de Pilatos

Plaza de Pilatos s/n, T954-225298. Daily 0900-1900, to 1800 winter. €12 lower floor, €18 both floors, free Wed from 1500 for EU citizens.

This stunning mansion is still partly inhabited by members of the family of the Dukes of Medinaceli, who built most of it in the late 15th to early 16th centuries. It owes its name to the story that the Duke, on a pilgrimage to Jerusalem, was so struck by the former residence of the Roman governors (including Pontius Pilate) that he decided to model his own house on it. The profusion of classical sculpture decorating the courtyards and gardens, some of it original, certainly gives the house a Roman air, but the architecture is principally an attractive blend of Renaissance classicism and *mudéjar* styles. Sensitive restoration has healed the damage caused during the Spanish Civil War.

The highlight of the visit is the central courtyard, reached from the entrance by passing under a thriving purple cascade of bougainvillea. It's a stunning combination of *azulejos* and stucco work; the Italianate central fountain is overseen by statues, including an excellent Athena Promachos. On the walls are mounted a series of Roman portrait heads, obtained by the dukes from Italy. The gardens are beautiful and peaceful; one even has a small grotto with tinkling water. The staircase to the upper level is a cascade of shining tiles topped by a majestic golden dome that owes some of its decoration to Moorish *mocárabes*.

Beyond here is accessed by a **guided tour** ⓘ *English and Spanish, tours leave hourly 1000-1800 except 1400*. The tour takes you through furnished rooms with some excellent 17th-century coffered ceilings and a large collection of paintings, including a Goya of the Ronda bullring.

Museo del Baile Flamenco

C Manuel Rojas Marcos 3, T954-340311, www.museoflamenco.com. Daily 1100-1800. Museum €6, show from €25.

This museum is devoted to flamenco dance and was founded by renowned *bailaora* Cristina Hoyos. Set in a lovely patioed building, it's a good spot to visit before you see some performances. There are stylish interactive displays on the world of flamenco dance, with an interestingly humanistic slant: dancers' lives are examined as well as the great performances. They have decent evening shows daily. There's also a shop and bar.

★Museo de Bellas Artes

Plaza del Museo 9, T954-786498. Tue-Sat 0900-2100, Sun 0900-1500. Free for EU citizens, €1.50 for others.

Seville's major art gallery is a must-see, picturesquely housed in a convent dating from the 17th and 18th centuries. This is appropriate enough, as most of the collection comes from the monasteries stripped of all their possessions in the Disentailment Act of 1835. The Sevillian school of painting was the dominant artistic force in Spain's Golden Age and is represented here in all its glory, offset by peaceful and pretty tiled patios.

The collection is thoughtfully laid out and thankfully uncluttered. Early pieces include a fine work from the monastery of San Agustín by Martín de Vos showing the awakening dead being sorted by angels and demons. In the same room there's also an El Greco – a good portrait of his own son.

In the early years of the 17th century, two distinct styles were evident in Sevillian painting, naturalism and mannerism, but these were gradually brought together as the century progressed. The latter style is well represented here by a selection of Francisco Pacheco's works. A portrait by the master Velázquez (Pacheco's son-in-law), of a gentleman against a brooding sky, is also in this section. Room IV has works of another mannerist, Alonso Vázquez, including, appropriately, a series on San Pedro Nolasco, who founded the original monastery on this site.

The former convent church is an awesome space with an elaborate painted ceiling. Here we see the evolution of the Seville school to its peak: the works of Zurbarán and Murillo. Although the former is represented here by an appropriately imposing heavenly Father and his large, famous Apotheosis of St Thomas Aquinas, there are more of his works upstairs; this room belongs to Murillo, whose statue graces the square outside the museum. Most of his works here are from the former Capuchin monastery. The city's patrons, Santa Justa and Santa Rufina, hold the Giralda in one renowned canvas, while a tender San Felix and child, *St Francis Embracing the Crucified Christ*, and the famous *Virgin of the Napkin*, who holds a wide-eyed Christ child, are other noteworthy pieces. While mannerist traces remain in his early work, Murillo evolves into a complete Baroque style characterised by intense religious fervour, usually centred on a gaze or glance of striking power or emotion.

There are more Murillos upstairs and a long gallery devoted to Juan de Valdés Leal (1622-1690). Zurbarán, a little out of context, is represented in Room X. In the corridor outside is perhaps his most powerful work here, a crucifixion of incredible solitude and force, with Christ, head-down, seemingly chiselled from rock.

The 19th- and 20th-century rooms have works by Sevillian proto-Impressionist Gonzalo Bilbao as well as a portrait of the haunted Romantic poet Gustavo Adolfo Bécquer, famously and sensitively portrayed by his brother Valeriano, while two good portraits by the Basque painter Ignacio Zuloaga and a fiesta scene by Gustavo Bacarisas round off the superb collection.

Basílica de Jesús del Gran Poder
Pl San Lorenzo 13, T954-915686, www.gran-poder.es. Oct-May Mon-Thu 0800-1330, 1730-2100, Fri 0730-2200, Sat-Sun 0900-1400, 1730-2100, Jun-Sep Mon-Thu 0800-1300, 1800-2100, Fri 0730-1400, 1700-2200, Sat-Sun 0900-1330, 1800-2100. Free.

This church has one of the city's most beloved Jesus statues. The 17th-century figure of Christ by Juan de Mesa, set in a side chapel, is a focus of local adoration and a breathtaking piece of art. Jesus looks utterly careworn and harrowed; the brotherhood's procession in the Madrugada is a Semana Santa highlight.

★ La Macarena
working-class barrio with Seville's best markets and buzzing nightlife

The large barrio of La Macarena, once one of the poorest slums in the peninsula, is an enticing web of narrow streets and numerous churches and chapels, occupying the northern portion of the old town. One church is home to Seville's best-loved Virgin, La Esperanza de la Macarena (known as La Macarena). She gives her name to many of Seville's women, one of whom was the subject of the bestselling Latin hit of all time, by the ageing duo Los del Río. Still a working-class zone, La Macarena is home to much of Seville's alternative culture. It's still demarcated by a long section of the city wall, the best-preserved chunk of what was once one of Europe's mightiest bastions.

Walking tour of Barrio La Macarena
Heading into the barrio along Calle Santa Clara, and then right up Calle Santa Ana, you reach the **Alameda de Hércules**. This long avenue lined with planes and poplars is the centre of Seville's alternative scene. Once a marsh, it was drained in the 16th century and adorned at both ends with Roman columns; upon the two southern columns were placed sculptures of Hercules, who is said to have founded Seville, and Julius Caesar, whose presence as governor of the province is considerably more certain. Every second Sunday of the month (Sep-Jun) there's a craft market here, while Seville's busiest and oldest flea market, El Jueves, takes place on Thursday mornings, a couple of blocks away on Calle Feria.

From the Alameda, follow Calle Peral, and then turn right up Calle Bécquer. This will bring you to the **Basílica de la Macarena** ⓘ *C Bécquer 1, T954-901800, daily 0900-1400, 1700-2100 (Jul to mid-Sep from 1800; Semana Santa 0900-1500 most days), free (€5 for museum)*, the home of arguably Seville's most-adored Mary and a fairly recent construction; the first stone was laid by Pope Pius XII in the 1940s. The Virgin takes pride of place in the *retablo*; the Christ from the other *paso* stands in front of her. You can see the *pasos* themselves in the museum, along with various gifts that have been bestowed on the Virgin and a variety of her garments.

Queipo de Llano, the general who ruled over Seville so brutally during the Civil War, was buried here, along with his wife Genoveva and right-hand man Francisco Bohórquez, until 2022. In keeping with the Ley de Memoria Democrática (Law of Democratic Memory), their remains were exhumed and returned to their families.

Across the main road from the basilica is the **Hospital de las Cinco Llagas**. Built in the 16th century, it is said to have been one of the biggest hospitals in Europe at the time. The sober façade is long and impressive but these days the patients have been replaced by politicians; it's the seat of Andalucía's regional parliament. On the main road here begins the best-preserved stretch of the city walls. They were originally at least partially Roman, perhaps built by Julius Caesar when he governed the region. The Moors made them formidable again, with the circumference of some 6 km defended by 166 towers, a moat and jagged castellation.

Back at the basilica, take Calle San Luis, which meanders its way back towards the centre of town. You soon pass **Plaza del Pumarejo**, a shady spot frequented by some real barrio characters, then the **Iglesia de Santa Marina**, with a *mudéjar* tower. Shortly afterwards, on the right you come to the **Iglesia de San Luis de los Franceses** ⓘ *C San Luis 27, T954-550207, Tue-Sun 1000-1400, 1600-2000, €4, audio guide €3,* whose flamboyant façade will snap you out of any heat-induced reverie. Although the road's too narrow to really appreciate the architecture, the front is a Baroque masterpiece with scores of Churrigueresque features; architect Leonardo de Figueroa also built El Salvador church and Palacio San Telmo. Inside the circular interior are several *retablos*, the finest of which is the main one, inlaid with blue ceramic and centred around a small Madonna painting; look out also for the massive Zurbarán painting depicting the saint-king Louis XIV of France in his earthly days. The ceiling frescoes in the dome are also very impressive; an ornate mirror is on hand to help you appreciate them.

Further down the street, the **Iglesia de San Marcos** is a Gothic-*mudéjar* church that was once a mosque. It has a well-crafted façade, with a toothed Gothic portal, delicate *mudéjar* blind arcading above, and the bearded evangelist himself atop. However, it is most notable for its slim tower, which is very similar in style to the Giralda. It's adorned with attractive brickwork and a series of windows that increase in size as the tower rises. Cervantes was fond of climbing to the top. The interior features some horseshoe arches, preserved despite extensive Civil War damage.

Behind the church, along Calle Santa Paula, is the **Convento de Santa Paula** ⓘ *C Santa Paula s/n, T635-131373, Tue-Sat 1000-1300, Sun 1030-1300, €6.* There's an air of mystery about a visit here; knock at the door and you'll eventually be admitted and get shown around by a knowledgeable old nun with a twinkle in her eye. It's the home of a few dozen nuns; the building dates from the 15th century and contains many pieces of art of varying quality and some fine faded, but wholly original, 15th-century *artesonado* ceilings. There's a gorgeous patio and a fine tiled doorway, a work of Pisano. On either side of the church is a pair of excellent sculptures by Martínez Montañés of the two Johns, while some Alonso Cano works are also present. Don't forget to buy some of the delicious Seville orange marmalade made by the nuns.

The clay-rich Isla de la Cartuja was a centre for potters' workshops in bygone centuries but was more or less derelict until the city decided to make it the site of the World Expo in 1992. Predictably for such an event, costs skyrocketed, and the city was left with massive debts and a huge space filled with modern buildings that needed to be used. Today it houses a science and technology park and is Seville's first low-emission zone. There's a popular theme park here, Isla Mágica; nearby the river is spanned by a number of bridges, most notably the supremely elegant Alamillo, designed by the Valencian architect Santiago Calatrava.

Monasterio de la Cartuja

Av Américo Vespucio 2, www.caac.es, Isla de la Cartuja, T955-037070. Tue-Sat 1100-2100, Sun 1000-1530. €1.80 for permanent collection or exhibition, €3 for both, free from 1900 weekdays and all day Sat.

The clay in this part of Seville meant that ceramics were made here from ancient times; it was in a pottery in the 13th century that the Virgin appeared and a shrine was built. It later became this important monastery, a favourite of Seville's wealthy and powerful in the Golden Age. Columbus came here to pray and contemplate his next voyages; after he died his remains lay here for 23 years.

In the Peninsular War, the arch-desecrator of Spanish cultural heritage, Marshal General Soult, stationed some troops here, and the buildings were badly damaged. Once the monks were expelled some 20 years later, it was in an extremely poor state and was picked up cheaply by Charles Pickman, a British businessman, who set up a ceramics factory on the site and lived there. Pickman generally respected the monastic buildings, though all were put to use, and the huge brick kilns and chimneys still dominate the site.

Renovated by the Sevillian authorities, it became the Royal Pavilion of Expo 92, and now houses a good contemporary art museum, the **Centro Andaluz de Arte Contemporáneo**. First visit the church itself, with a small cloister, a refectory with a beautiful coffered ceiling, and the well-carved tombs of the powerful Ribera family. Then access the galleries (the layout of the complex is confusing so pick up a map). The temporary exhibitions are usually good and the gallery spaces white, uncluttered and relaxing.

Selected works from the permanent collection – including many Andalucian artists – will be housed in the refurbished 15th-century pavilion from the 1992 Expo, opening mid-2026.

⭐ Itálica

Santiponce (9 km from Seville), T955-996583. Mid-Sep to Mar Tue-Sat 0900-1800, Sun 0900-1500; Apr to mid-Jun Tue-Thu 0900-1800, Fri-Sat 0900-2100, Sun 0900-1500; mid-Jul to mid-Sep Tue-Sun 0900-1500. Free EU citizens, otherwise €1.50. To get here, take the M-170A (www.damas-sa.es) bus from Plaza de Armas bus station to Santiponce, €2 each way (25 mins), every 30 mins weekdays and on Sat mornings, every hour on Sat afternoons and Sun; by car take the N630 north (following the signposts for Mérida) across the Puente Cristo de la Expiración.

It's hard to believe, wandering around the ruins of Itálica, that this was once one of the Roman Empire's largest and most influential cities. In truth, little of it has been excavated; what you can walk around today is the partially revealed remains of the *nova urbs* (new town; a relative term these days) built by Hadrian in the early second century AD, while the *vetus urbs* (old town) lies under the village of Santiponce. It was originally built by Publius Cornelius Scipio in 206 BC; one of the Italian (not Roman) regiments of his army had a rough time of it during the battle against the Carthaginians at Ilipa and he decided to build a settlement for them to let them heal up and ease the threat of mutiny. The first Roman conurbation in the Iberian peninsula, Itálica grew rapidly and in time became an important Roman city in the region, birthplace of the emperor Trajan and perhaps his protégé Hadrian, who certainly grew up here.

Your visit starts in the small visitor centre near the entrance, with a brief, context-setting film about Hadrian. The famous wall builder pimped up the city, adding lavish public baths, expanding the theatre and amphitheatre, and holding grand processions to honour the gods. Outside, head right for the main attraction: the huge amphitheatre which seated 25,000. Although much of the seating has been removed over the years, the terraces are still very clear, as are the stairways and the large sunken area in the middle (thought to have had a central dais erected over it for use in gladiatorial combats). One fascinating find is displayed in a side chamber: a bronze tablet inscribed with norms for gladiatorial combat imposed by Marcus Aurelius and his son (who else but Commodus, Russell Crowe's sworn enemy in *Gladiator*).

The other highlights are the mosaics on display on the floors of some of the excavated houses. The **House of Neptune**'s mosaic features sea creatures, including the god himself, while the outer edges depict a Nilotic hunting scene; it's not without its humour, as the large crane doing an injury to a hunter's backside attests. There's a statue of the god-emperor Trajan near here; this section of the city was built by Hadrian in his adoptive father's honour. The **House of the Birds** also has some excellent mosaics, two of which colourfully feature an array of the feathered tribe. The **House of the Planetarium** has perhaps the finest piece, with portraits of the seven divinities who gave their name to the Roman week.

Turn right out of the entrance and up the hill to check out the partially restored Roman theatre and the excellent visitor centre, Cotidiana Vitae, where you can imagine yourself as a Roman in 2nd century AD Itálica in a *taberna* (shop) and dining room with *lecti* (couches for reclining). An impressively immersive video imagines the city's streets in its heyday. Then head straight for the monastery further up the road. The return bus passes the entrance to this, so you won't have to retrace your steps.

The **Monasterio San Isidoro del Campo** ⓘ *T955-624400, mid-Sep to mid-Jun Tue-Thu 1000-1500, Fri-Sat 1000-1900, Sun 1000-1430, mid-Jun to mid-Sep Tue-Sun 1000-1430*, was founded in 1301 by Guzmán El Bueno in the place where, by tradition, San Isidoro (St Isidore) had been interred until the removal of his remains to León. It's a sizeable monastery whose imposing walls attest to its double function as a fortress in those uncertain times. The place has had an interesting history; one of its monastic communities dabbled in translations of forbidden texts, not a healthy move in 16th-century Spain with the Inquisition at the peak of its power and paranoia about Protestantism rife. Some of the monks fled the country, others were burned for their bookish crimes. Guzmán and his wife are buried in the curious twin church, alongside a magnificent *retablo* by Martínez Montañés. One of the cloisters features unusual *mudéjar* frescoes.

Alcalá de Guadaira

Now basically a suburb of Seville, the friendly town of Alcalá is worth visiting for its huge, muscular Almohad fortress. It's very impressive, if a shell; little remains inside the walls. The M122 bus runs every 15-30 minutes from San Bernardo; €1.20.

Feedback request

At Bradt Guides we're aware that guidebooks start to go out of date on the day they're published – and that you, our readers, are out there in the field doing research of your own. You'll find out before us when a fine new family-run hotel opens or a favourite restaurant changes hands and goes downhill. So why not tell us about your experiences?

Contact us on **01753 893444** or **info@bradtguides.com**. We will forward emails to the author who may post updates on the Bradt website at bradtguides. com/updates. Alternatively, you can add a review of the book to Amazon, or share your adventures with us on Facebook, X or Instagram (**@BradtGuides**).

Tourist information

Sevilla City Tourist Office
Paseo Marqués de Contadero, T954-471232, Mon-Sun 0930-1830.
Apart from this main tourist office by the river (next to the *Nao Victoria* ship), there are also offices at the Costurero de la Reina (small striped building next to María Luisa Park) and in Castillo San Jorge in Triana (by the bridge). In addition, you'll find Junta de Andalucía booths at the airport and at platform 6 at Santa Justa train station. The **Seville Pass**, www.seville-pass.com, includes cathedral and Alcázar entry, and hop-on hop-off or airport bus. It also Includes an audio guide to the city. It costs €48, slightly less online.

Where to stay

There's a wealth of choice of attractive and intimate lodgings set in beautifully renovated Sevillian mansions.
  If you're planning a visit in spring, booking ahead is essential. All places raise their prices massively during Semana Santa and the Feria. The widest choice of well-priced self-catering apartments is on airbnb.com, but we've listed a few notable recommendations. Price codes here reflect high season (but not Semana Santa or Feria) prices.

The cathedral and around

€€€€ Alfonso XIII
C San Fernando 2, T954-917000, www.hotel-alfonsoxiii-sevilla.com.
One of Spain's most luxurious historic hotels, this huge neo-Moorish building was erected for the 1929 exhibition. It

is beautifully decorated with opulent patios. The hotel is 5-star in every sense, but the prices are predictably high, especially during Seville's festive season. You'll get the best deals via the website.

€€€€ Eme Catedral Mercer Hotel
C Alemanes 27, T954-560000, www.emecatedralmercerhotel.com.
This fashion-conscious modern hotel by the cathedral brought a splash of modern design to Seville's old centre. Certain humorous touches, undeniably attractive furnishings, and enticing features like the small rooftop pool and multilevel bar win it points; the rooms are stylish but perhaps lack features for this price. The location is wonderful.

€€€ U-Sense Sevilla Centro
C Álvarez Quintero 52, T954-293913, www.urbansense.es.
On this likeable pedestrian street linking the cathedral with Plaza del Salvador, this hotel trades in warm personal service; with only 11 rooms, it feels like they've got time for all their guests. The rooms are spacious, modern, and sparklingly clean, with efficient a/c and really good bathrooms. There's no parking particularly close.

€€ TOC Hostel Sevilla
Miguel Mañara 18, T954-501244, www.tochostels.com.
It's hard to find fault with this brilliant spot slap-bang in the heart of the main monument area. It's got both private en suite rooms and comfortable dorms, all with upbeat modern décor and thoughtful design features. The staff have a helpful attitude. Great features

include the reception area and the back terrace. Recommended.

Barrio Santa Cruz

€€€€ Casa del Poeta

C Don Carlos Alonso Chaparro 3, T954-213868, www.casadelpoeta.es.
With a very discreet entrance in the heart of Santa Cruz (the street is a little cul-de-sac off Ximénez Enciso), this is another heart-stoppingly beautiful Seville patio hotel. Rooms are elegant and unfussily handsome – we loved the duplex one – and staff are professional and eager to please. Recommended.

€€€€ Corral del Rey

Corral del Rey 12, T954-227116, www.corraldelrey.com.
This boutique hotel turned heads in the Spanish hotel world for its faultlessly realised restoration of a historic *palacio*, its irresistible romantic ambience, thoughtfully selected modern art, and its beautiful rooms, which are coupled with excellent bathrooms and equipped with all sorts of amenities. There's a gourmet restaurant here, and a small rooftop pool; the staff are commendably solicitous. Further rooms and suites in two annexes opposite are equally delightful. Recommended.

€€€€ El Rey Moro

C Reinoso 8, T622-277336, www.elreymoro.com.
Run by the restaurant of the same name, this excellent hotel that sits between 3 central Santa Cruz streets is built around a magnificent 3-storey patio with wooden columns. The appealing rooms have beams, big beds and shiny modern bathrooms; some face inwards on to the patio, others face the street and the buzz of the Plaza de los Venerables restaurants. Staff are charming, and provide free bicycles; there's also free afternoon tea.

€€€€ Las Casas de la Judería

C Santa María La Blanca, T954-415150, www.lascasasdelajuderiasevilla.com.
This vast yet intimate hotel complex spreads across several old *palacios* in the Barrio Santa Cruz – all have been superbly renovated, with sparkling patios, pretty nooks, and hanging foliage. The rooms are sizeable, luxurious enough and agreeable, though a little dark and stuffy. Service is conscientious and there's live music in the piano bar every evening. A particular highlight of the hotel is the originally decorated underground passageway to the dining room and spa; the rooftop pool is also a plus. Recommended.

€€€ Hotel Amadeus & La Música

C Farnesio 6, T954-501443, www.hotelamadeussevilla.com.
A fantastic and original hotel occupying 4 adjacent buildings with a musical theme. The individually decorated rooms are named after composers; some have a piano, of which there are also a couple downstairs. All rooms have first-rate facilities. A highlight, apart from the charming service, is the spacious roof terrace with views over the centre, including the Giralda. Highly recommended.

€ Hotel Goya

C Mateos Gago 31, T954-211170, www.hotelgoyasevilla.com.
Located at the top of the street that is Seville's tapas epicentre, the Goya is

a cool place with marbled floors and a/c. The rooms are large and fairly minimalist, with excellent bathrooms. Some have balconies overlooking this interesting street.

€ Pensión San Pancracio
Plaza de las Cruces 9, T954-413104, pensionsanpancracio@hotmail.com.
In a tucked-away nook of the barrio, this is a good cheap choice; a touch faded, but well-scrubbed and quiet. There are several room choices: they are all adequate, with light and air from a central patio. The bathrooms are shared and clean. Ground-floor rooms are cooler, but those above have a fan (one double has a/c); take your pick.

Self-catering
Numbers of tourist apartments have been limited by the city council, but there are many in Barrio Santa Cruz listed online on sites such as www. booking.com and www.airbnb.com.

€€€€ Hotels and Suites Murillo
C Lope de Rueda 16, T954-216095, www.hotelmurillo.com.
As well as two hotels in the heart of Barrio Santa Cruz, **Hotel Murillo** also runs stylish modern apartments in three nearby locations (Plaza Alfaro, and by the cathedral and Alcázar). The curved corner balcony on Plaza Alfaro is one of Seville's most romantic spots.

Triana

€€€ Hotel Monte Triana
C Clara de Jesús Montero 24, T954-343111, www.hotel-montetriana.com.
With a barrio location in Triana but close to the bus station and bridge, this makes an appealing and somewhat

secluded Seville base; the rooftop pool and terrace are glorious. Staff are excellent and the modern rooms are very well kept. The buffet breakfast is better than average too.

€ Triana Backpackers Hostel
C Rodrigo de Triana 69, T954-459960, www.trianahostel.com.
This backpackers' hostel stands out for its Triana location as well as traveller-friendly features such as free internet, breakfast and a roof terrace with a jacuzzi. It's a sociable place with friendly staff and a welcoming feel. It's not the cheapest, and couples won't get value from the cramped doubles, but it's a great place to meet other folk.

El Arenal

€€€ Hotel Adriano
C Adriano 12, T954-293800, www.adrianohotel.com.
This boutique hotel has a great location near the bullring and in the heart of a great tapas and restaurant area. Décor is in keeping with the building's 18th-century origins, with antique furniture and gilt trim. There's parking available too, and a rooftop bar.

€€ Hotel Simón
C García de Vinuesa 19, T954-226660, www.hotelsimonsevilla.com.
Long a Seville favourite, this is an attractive hotel built around a beautiful airy courtyard with a fountain. There are plenty of *azulejos* and neo-Moorish features. Rooms are smallish but accommodating and decorated as thoughtfully as the rest of the establishment. It's not luxurious, but good value for the décor and ambience.

Centro and San Vicente

€€€€ Las Casas del Rey de Baeza

Plaza Jesús de la Redención 2, off C Santiago, T954-561496, www.hospes.com.

An enchanting place to stay near Casa de Pilatos, this old *corral de vecinos* has been superbly restored to be charming but not overdone. The patios are surrounded by pretty wooden galleries and the hessian rugs are a great touch. The rooms are big, with huge beds and all facilities. Guests have a rooftop pool and terrace as well as an elegantly decorated library and lounges. The service is first rate; good restaurant too. Recommended.

€€€ Las Casas de los Mercaderes

C Álvarez Quintero 9, T955-136211, www.sercotel.com.

In the heart of the shopping district and a short walk from the centre is this contemporary-styled hotel. The rooms are simply furnished and spacious, with smart TVs; the hotel is built around a striking red-and-white arcaded patio with stained-glass roof.

€€ Hostal Museo

C Abad Gordillo 17, T954-915526, www.hommuseo.com.

Offering excellent value for money, this clean and courteously run place is a short stroll from the bus station and very close to the Fine Arts Museum. There are flawless, comfortable rooms, across 3 (joined) buildings.

€€ Santiago 15

C Santiago 15, T955-318066, www.santiago15.nuahotels.com.

Close to the tapas bars of Plaza Terceros, this converted mansion has a welcoming feel with potted palms, pretty tiled floors and bright, modern rooms. Upper floors get less traffic noise.

Self-catering

€€€€ Palacio Bucarelli

C Dalia 1, T696-167188, www.palaciobucarelli.com.

These spacious, elegant apartments sleeping 2 to 3 are part of a family-owned palace in San Vicente. There's a gorgeous wisteria-covered bower and small shared pool. Breakfast is delivered to your door. Recommended.

La Macarena

The Macarena barrio, particularly around the Alameda de Hércules, is a good spot to be based if you want to explore the less touristy parts of old Seville; there are great tapas and nightlife and no camera-toting hordes.

€€€€ Casa Romana

C Trajano 15, T954-915170, www.hotelcasaromana.com.

Well-located between the Alameda and the city's Roman past with repro busts dotted about its main building and annexe opposite. Rooms are well sized and light, and superiors have hydro-massage baths. Recommended.

€€€ Hotel Alcoba del Rey

C Bécquer 9, T954-915800, www.alcobadelrey.com.

Close to the home of the Virgen de Macarena, this charming hotel offers cordial service and plentiful facilities at the northern edge of the old town. The décor is Moroccan-inspired, with attractive imported furniture lending a North African ambience. Every room is stylish and distinct, with unusual bathroom design providing plenty of romance and charm. The best of the rooms has a candlelit jacuzzi; a honeymoon special.

€€€ Patio de la Alameda

Alameda de Hércules 56, T954-904999, www.patiodelaalameda.com.

This classy hotel makes a top-value place to stay. Built around 2 striking terracotta-coloured patios, it has excellent rooms and a pleasant rooftop bar. The location right on the Alameda de Hércules is great for strolling and bar-hopping. Recommended.

€ Hostal Macarena

C San Luis 91, T954-370141, www. hostalmacarenasevilla.com.

Great budget option on Plaza del Pumarejo; friendly, family-run and set around a lovely atrium, with beautiful tile-work and cheerful blue-and-yellow décor. Rooms come with or without bath.

Restaurants

There's sometimes little distinction between restaurants and tapas bars in Seville; most restaurants include an area to stand and snack, while at tapas bars you can usually sit down and order meal-sized portions (*raciones*). Accepted practice is to stand at the bar, have a couple of tapas and also taste what your friends are eating. A standard tapa will cost €4-6. Tapas portions and set menus virtually disappear during Semana Santa when restaurants and bars are full to bursting.

The cathedral and around

€ Cervecería Giralda

C Mateos Gago, T954-228250, cerveceriagiralda.es.

A stone's throw from the cathedral on this buzzing pedestrianised street – soak up tower views from its pavement terrace. The vaulted, painted roof, with star-shaped holes and coloured motifs from an Arabic bath, was discovered during a 2020 revamp. An extraordinary space, though the tapas are average.

Barrio Santa Cruz

The lovely Barrio Santa Cruz is an obvious place to eat, with its shady plazas and terraces. Unfortunately, a high percentage of the restaurants are aimed at tourists, and serve below-par food at inflated prices.

€€ Casa Román

Pl de los Venerables 1, T954-228483, www.casaromansevilla.com.

Sit outside under the orange trees in the pretty square, or admire the hanging *jamones* (hams) and romantic paintings inside. Renowned for its *chacinas* (cold meats), but staples like *espinacas con garbanzos* (spinach with chickpeas) are also reliable. Gets busy, so arrive when it opens at 8pm.

€€ Las Teresas

C Santa Teresa 2, T954-213069, www.lasteresas.es.

Research indicates that 9 out of 10 people dredge up an image very similar to this Santa Cruz local when they think of the words 'tapas bar'. Hams: check, tiles: check, patina of age: check, gruff but lovable bar staff: check, mouth-watering smell of fried fish: check. Popular with locals and visitors. Recommended.

€€ Vinería San Telmo

Paseo Catalina de Ribera 4, T954-410600, www.vineriasantelmo.com.

A firm favourite with locals and visitors alike, with a sizeable terrace and consistently excellent service, this place serves up imaginative salads, creative, well-executed dishes, and delectable desserts (lemon meringue pie, flourless chocolate torte), plus an impressive wine list. An all-round winner.

€ Bar Alfalfa
Corner C Alfalfa and C Candilejo, T954-222344.
On the square of the same name, this excellent Italian tapas bar is decorated with farming implements, earthenware jars and hundreds of bottles of wine. Enjoy a perfect *bruschetta* here, divine *bresaola* or a selection of Italian cheeses. You can order streetside on warm evenings. Recommended.

€ Bodega Santa Cruz
C Rodrigo Caro 1, T954-218618.
This busy and cheerful bar does some of Seville's choicest tapas and *montaditos*, with *cazón en adobo* or *pringá* particularly delicious. As the night wears on, the frantically busy bar staff wipe what they've run out of off the menus, which are chalked up at each end of the bar. Sees plenty of tourists but still very authentic. Also known as **Las Columnas**. Recommended.

€ La Goleta Taberna Álvaro Peregil
C Mateos Gago 20, T954-218966.
Simple, tiny bar with loads of atmosphere. Run by a notable local character, it's a historic Santa Cruz watering hole. It specialises in a tasty orange wine; the tapas are limited but excellent. Humorous touches abound, and when the boss Alvaro's on form it's a one-man show. There's a more spacious extension open next door but the original is best.

Triana
C Betis that runs along the river is full of places to eat and drink, not all of them good. C San Jacinto is pedestrianised and has some reliably excellent options.

€€€ Abades Triana
C Betis 69, T954-286459, www.abadestriana.com.
This riverfront restaurant occupies a hard-to-miss modern building that's all glass and light, offering wonderful views over the Guadalquivir and across to the Moorish Torre del Oro. The food is high-priced, but there are some very tasty fish dishes and an inventive tapas tasting menu. The location is especially seductive at night.

€€ La Blanca Paloma
C Jacinto 49, T954-333640, www.blancapalomatriana.es.
This cheerful Triana venue was always one of the best tapas stops this side of the Guadalquivir. It has the same boisterous bar scene and also offers an excellent restaurant, with the philosophy of originality combined with good humour and high-quality ingredients. Try the *bacalao al horno* (baked cod with a prawn sauce).

€ Bar Santa Ana
C Pureza 82, T954-239265, facebook.com/barsantaanatriana.
A neighbourhood stalwart for decades, close to the adored La Esperanza's church, this place has retained its friendly local character while updating the menu – the *patatas bravas* are legendary.

El Arenal

€€ Bodeguita Antonio Romero
C Antonia Díaz 19, T954-223939.
Cheery waistcoated waiters man the bar at this warm and inviting venue. It's got a very typical feel, and serves up delicious tapas like *montadito de pringá*, a succulent stewed meat sandwich. There are several offshoots nearby.

€€ La Brunilda
C Galera 5, T954 220481,
www.labrunildatapas.com.
Exposed brick and a backstreet location give this a romantic feel … or they would, if it weren't a trendy Seville bar on the food hound circuit. The tapas are great, featuring fresh market produce with refreshing twists, but expect to queue: not just for a table, but even to get to the bar.

€€ La Cata
C Pavia 12, T854-521209.
Neighbourhood wine bar with a warm welcome, inventive tapas, fab daily specials (stewed wild boar cheeks) and a great selection of local wines (recommended: Bodegas Salado).

€ Bar Pepe Hillo
C Adriano 24, T954-564145.
A legend in its own tapas-time, this place is always full to bursting with animated *sevillanos* enjoying their tasty stews and *croquetas* among other goodies. A pork *solomillo* in sweet wine and raisin sauce is another star. High ceilinged, busy and buzzy, it's decorated with farming implements and no fewer than 10 bulls' heads lugubriously observe proceedings. There's a very attractive dining area out the back, away from the hurly-burly of the bar.

€ Casa Morales
C García de Vinuesa 11, T954-221242.
This great old place is in a one-time bodega – the vast jars in the rear bar used to hold the wine. The service is old style, with knowledgeable, friendly chat. The *montaditos* are served on a wee wooden board; the *guiso del día* (stew of the day) is often a tempting option. Recommended.

€ Casa Moreno
C Gamazo 7,
www.casamorenosevilla.com.
Hidden away just off Plaza Nueva, this place is a Seville institution. Stand at the bar as they prep delicious little grilled sandwiches – try the *chorizo picante con queso cabrales* (spicy chorizo with blue cheese). Extremely busy at weekends.

Centro and San Vicente

€€ Bodega Góngora
C Albareda 5, T954-219119,
www.bodegagongora.com.
Named after a local winery, whose wines they sell, this is an atmospheric bar where third-generation owner Cuqui serves up classic tapas like pork cheeks in Pedro Ximénez, *adobo* (marinated dogfish) and *ortiguillas* (sea anenomes); the grilled anchovies are delectable. Good sherries too. Note, only large plates are served at tables outside; for tapas, stay inside at the bar.

€€ Taberna Zurbarán
Pl de Zurbarán 2, instagram.com/ tabernazurbaran.
The orange tree-lined square close to Las Setas which serves as the large terrace of this taberna makes it a popular central spot. Menu staples include tangy *gildas* (little pintxos of olive, spicy pepper and anchovy) and lamb skewers; the tortilla is particularly renowned. Daily specials (on the board) might include quail, rabbit or partridge. Inside there are tall tables and stools.

€ El Rinconcillo
C Gerona 40, T954-223183,
www.elrinconcillo.es.
An incredibly old bar that was founded in 1670 when the Habsburgs still ruled

Spain. It's an attractive place that's definitely worth a visit. The fittings are all wooden and the hams hanging over the counter look as old as the bar. The tapas are good and served until fairly late; the *croquetas* are particularly memorable.

€ La Antigua Bodeguita
Plaza del Salvador 6, T954-561833.
As long as the weather holds, the interior of this popular bar is just a place to order, as the crowd from here and the bar next door spills out on to the square. It's a great Sevillian scene in its own right, but the tapas are also worthy, particularly the seafood. Check out *mojama*, cured tuna meat, which will either delight or disgust.

Cafés

La Campana
C Sierpes 1, T954-223570, www.confiterialacampana.com.
An institution in this part of town, this place will seduce the sweet-toothed with its ice creams and pastries. During Semana Santa, when it's *the* place to have a seat booked, it has an impressive display of pointy caramel *nazarenos*. At other times, try the *yemas* or the *lenguas de almendra*.

La Macarena

€€€ El Disparate
Alameda de Hércules 11, T680-127413, www.somoseldisparate.com.
Highly creative dishes on a buzzing terrace that is a prime viewing point for Alameda life. Dishes are small but exquisitely presented, with tantalising flavour combinations: prawn tartare with almond and coconut soup; pork cheek in Oloroso sherry with sweet potato, spinach and edamame. The

wine list will delight lovers of sherry and sparkling wines, but is strong in all areas. Great service.

€€ Yebra
C Medalla Milagrosa 3, T954-351007, www.yebrarestauracion.com. Closed Sun night and Mon.
Just outside the walls beyond the edge of Macarena barrio, this is one of Seville's best tapas joints; a smart but relaxed place offering authentic and original gourmet tapas at around €5-6. It's not often that you'll see partridge or pheasant on tapas menus, but you do here. The only drawback is its popularity; getting an order in can be a nightmare.

€ Condendê
Mercado Feria, C Feria 98, T623-035530, facebook.com/condende.
Brazilian-owned eatery that occupies a growing section of Feria market. Lively, casual vibe and eclectic menu of *gyozas*, *empanadas*, *arepas* and samosas, with tasty fillings catering for all dietary persuasions. Drink Godello white wine or locally made kombucha.

Bars and clubs

Seville's nightlife can't compete in terms of variety with Barcelona or Madrid, but you certainly won't be left sipping vodka in an empty bar. Seville folk tend to call it a night fairly early midweek and party until sun-up come the weekend, but there are plenty of zones that are always lively, particularly around Plaza Alfalfa in the old town and C Betis in Triana, both populated by a mixture of locals and tourists. Rooftop terrace bars are a great option, especially on hot summer nights. Most high-end hotels have them; some offer live music.

Bars

Bulebar Café
Alameda de Hércules 83, T689-497338, facebook.com/BulebarCafe.
One of several good choices on this long promenade, the Bulebar is colourfully decorated and has a great terrace shaded by a jasmine-covered bower. It's a popular meeting point for an alternative set.

Kiosco del Agua
Paseo de Colón 10, T609-293386, facebook.com/kioscodelagua.
On the riverfront across the road from the Teatro Maestranza, this is one of Seville's best spots for an evening beer. Sit on the wrought-metal chairs and watch the sun set over Triana while bats and swallows flutter among the silhouetted palm trees. Good views of the floodlit Torre del Oro too.

Embarcadero
C Betis 69B, T954-285001, facebook.com/ el.embarcaderotriana. Mon-Thu 1600-0100, Fri-Sat 1600-0200, Sun 1600-2100.
Right next to the river (the entrance is easy to miss), this relaxed place with beachy canvas and wooden chairs is a great place to while away the afternoon watching the boats chug past.

The Second Room
C Placentines 19, T603-628759. Open 1500-0200 or 0300.
Great *copas*, cocktails and mojitos served by waiting staff who don't seem to have the usual attitude problem – in fact, they look pleased to be here. Top views of the Giralda.

Clubs

Antique Theatro
C Matemáticos Rey Pastor y Castro s/n,
T954-462207, www.antiquetheatro.com. Daily Jun-Sep, Thu-Sun Oct-May. Open 2330-0600/0700, but don't turn up until at least 0300 unless you want the place to yourself. Cover charge €10-25 with a drink; sometimes free entry before 0130.
Seville's most upmarket nightclub, with an excellent sound system and committed DJs in one of the old pavilions from the 1992 Expo.

Fun Club
Alameda de Hércules 84, T650-800100, www.funclubsevilla.com. Thu-Sat 2400-0600 or so (2100 or so if live band playing). Entry is around €5 or often free otherwise (€7-15 for gig).
A music venue and *discoteca* with some serious alternative cred in these parts. There's often live rock, drum 'n' bass or good DJs.

Groucho
C Federico Sánchez Bedoya 22, 1954-228893, www.grouchobar.com.
This stylish *discoteca* tucked away on an Arenal side street is definitely one of the city's spots to be seen. There are 2 rooms and 3 VIP areas; be prepared to queue at weekends.

Itaca
C Amor de Dios 31, facebook.com/ itacadisco.
Seville's best-established gay *discoteca*, always well attended, and with appropriately good dance music. There's a backroom, and shows Wed-Sat nights.

Entertainment

Your best guide to upcoming events is the magazine *El Giraldillo*, www. elegirhoy.com; www.yuzin.com (print and online), www.onsevilla.com and www.sevillsecreta.co are also worth checking out for cultural events.

Cinema

Check www.ecartelera.com/cartelera for what's on.

Avenida 5 Cines, *C Marqués de Paradas 15, T954-293025*. Original-version films subtitled in Spanish.

Flamenco

Whether you're planning to spend every hour of darkness trawling bars in search of the most authentic *cante jondo* or just want to briefly experience what it's all about, it's likely that you'll want to see some flamenco when you're in Seville. While much of what's on offer is geared to tourists (although frequently of a very high technical standard), it's still possible to track down a more authentic experience.

There are essentially 3 ways to see flamenco in Seville. The *tablaos* are organised performances in set venues, with entry ranging from €20 to €35. The crowd at these is mostly tourists, the performers often well known and of a very high standard, and there are two or three shows every evening, each lasting around an hour.

Secondly, there are flamenco *peñas*, which are local members' clubs for aficionados. These have lower prices, and some seats are reserved for members.

Thirdly, in bars where flamenco enthusiasts hang out – and there are still plenty in Triana – you may see some impromptu performances. The tourist office has a fuller list of shows and flamenco bars.

Auditorio Álvarez Quintero, *C Álvarez Quintero 48, T605-130130, www.tablao alvarezquintero.com*. Daily evening shows at 1900 and 2045, among the most authentic of the *tablaos*. €25 entry.

Teatro Flamenco de Triana, *C Pureza 76, Triana, T611-002330, www.teatroflamencotriana.com*. Like most shows listed here, these have 2 singers, a male and female dancer, plus guitarist. 2 to 3 performances per night (3 from March to October and at Christmas), €25. The theatre is owned by the next-door flamenco school, Fundación Cristina Heeren ⓘ www. flamencoheeren.com; after watching the pros in action, try a class.

Casa de la Memoria, *C Cuna 6, T954-560670, www.casadelamemoria.es*. 4 nightly shows of good quality at this venue in central Seville. They cost €24; this is decent value, because the performers are usually first-class and the atmosphere intimate; be sure to book in advance as it's a small venue.

La Carbonería, *C Céspedes 21, T954-229945, www.lacarbonerialevies.blogspot. com. Open 1900-0100*. Long-established, popular bar, a former coal yard (hence the name) where flamenco is performed at 2330 every night. It's very touristy, but there's sometimes a strong gypsy presence too, and some of the flamenco is very good. Free (but the drinks are slightly pricier than normal).

Los Gallos, *Plaza de Santa Cruz 11, Barrio Santa Cruz, T954-216981, www.tablao losgallos.com*. This is a touristy *tablao* but definitely one of the best of its kind, with high-quality performers. There are 2 shows a night; go to the later one. €38 including a drink.

Museo del Baile Flamenco, *C Manuel Rojas Marcos 3, T954-340311, www. museoflamenco.com*. Live performances by exceptional artists every night. 4 shows daily (€25): 1 at 1200 in busier months, and 3 in the evening. Book ahead and arrive early to get a seat near the front.

Music
The main venues for classical concerts are the theatres (see below). For live music, see also Bars and clubs, above, and Flamenco, above. *El Giraldillo* is the best guide to upcoming performances.

Theatre
These theatres put on a range of drama, music and dance.
La Fundición, *Casa de la Moneda, C Habana 18, T954-225844, www. fundiciondesevilla.es.* In the attractively refurbished complex that was once the royal mint, this has a variety of comedy, flamenco, dance and other theatre.
Teatro Lope de Vega, *Av María Luisa, T955-472828, www.teatrolopedevega.org.* This lovely building constructed for the 1929 exhibition is currently closed, due to reopen in Sep 2026.
Teatro Maestranza, *Paseo de Cristóbal Colón 22, T954-223344, www.teatrodela maestranza.es.* This acclaimed modern building is Seville's main venue for

opera, drama and dance. The ticket office is open Mon-Sat 1000-1400, 1700-2000; it's a fairly dressy scene.

Festivals

It's well worth planning your trip to coincide with the solemn Semana Santa processions or the subsequent Feria de Abril, but you'll be paying more for accommodation and should reserve rooms well in advance.

5 Jan Cabalgata de los Reyes Magos, is a colourful parade of the 3 kings through the streets. They travel in colourful carriages and toss sweets and gifts to onlookers.
Easter Semana Santa (29 Mar-5 Apr 2026, 21-28 Mar 2027, 9-16 Apr 2028). The most famous of Spain's celebrations is in Seville. Members of the city's 60 *cofradías* parade *pasos* of Christ and the Virgin through the city streets. See box, page 18.
Apr Feria de Abril is the major social event of the Seville calendar. Upwards of 1000 *casetas* (striped tents) see a week of eating, drinking and parading their pretty horse carriages and *flamenca* dresses. See box, page 26.
Sep (even years only) **Bienal de Flamenco** is a major flamenco event, held in various venues around the city. Check www.labienal.com for information.
Around 8 Dec In the **Fiesta de la Inmaculada**, *tunas* (traditional student minstrel bands) gather at night in the Plaza del Triunfo to sing traditional songs. In the morning, children perform the *Danza de los Seises* in the cathedral (the dance is also performed at Corpus Christi in late May to mid-Jun).

Language schools and teachers

Instituto de Estudios de la Lengua Española (IELE), C García de Vinuesa 29, T954-560788, www.iele.com, is a popular school; **SevillaELE**, T611-171527, www.sevillaele.com, is not a school, but teacher Cristina Ramos focuses on learning in real-life situations; **CLIC**, C Albareda 19, T954-502131, www.clic.es, is a frequently recommended school with lively teaching, small class sizes and packages including accommodation and excursions.

Shopping

Books

Antonio Castro, *C Sol 3, T954-217030, www.castrolibros.es.* Nice old second-hand bookshop in the old town with a respectable selection of English paperbacks.

La Casa del Libro, *C Velázquez 8, T911-793463, www.casadellibro.com.* Good large bookshop for any needs, including travel or English language.

Ceramics

If it's superb ceramics or ceramic tiles you're after, Triana is the place to go. There are several attractively decorated shops, some of which have been family run for generations. Most of these shops are used to tourists and can arrange reasonably priced secure international delivery. If you're not an EU resident, pick up an IVA-exemption form with any major purchase, see page 105.

Ceramica Triana, *C Callao 14, T954-332179, www.ceramicatriana.com.* One of a few excellent ceramic shops in Triana.

Populart, *C Pasaje de Vila 4, T954-229444, www.populartsevilla.com.* Outstanding selection of antique hand-painted ceramics, including beautiful *lebrillo* bowls and centuries-old tiles. A rarity in streets near the cathedral largely lined with units flogging mass-produced tourist tat.

Clothes and fashion

Seville's main shopping zone is around **C Sierpes**, **C Tetuán**, **C Velázquez**, **C Cuna** and **Plaza del Duque**. This busy area is the place to come for clothes, be it well-priced modern Spanish gear, or essential Seville Feria fashion: shawls, *flamenca* dresses, ornamental combs, jewellery and fans.

For more offbeat shopping, head to the area south of the Alameda, and around C Pérez Galdós.

Department stores

El Corte Inglés, *Plaza Duque de la Victoria 8, T954-597000, C San Pablo 1, T954-597000, Av Luis Montoto 122 (Nervión), T954-571445, www.elcorte ingles.es.* Spain's premier department store, with almost anything you could want to buy. Excellent gourmet food sections at Duque and Nervión.

Food and drink

Inés Rosales, *Pl de San Francisco 15, T954-227281.* Famous *tortas de aceite* (olive oil biscuits) and traditional sweets, plus great local wines, olive oil, marmalade and superior tinned goods, with hand-luggage friendly 100 ml bottles and jars. Helpful staff.

Markets

The big Thu flea market, **El Jueves**, takes place on C Feria and is one of Europe's oldest, with stalls selling antiques, ceramics, clothes, toys and other collectibles. **Paseo del Arte** artisan market takes place on Sun on the pretty Triana riverfront. There are excellent food markets in **Triana** by the Puente Isabel II, in **El Arenal** and also on **C Feria**.

What to do

Bike hire

Bike stands are all over the centre, with a €2.59 daily/€13.33 weekly fee plus around €1-2 per hour (free for the first 30 mins). See www.sevici.es for details.

Bici4City, *Antonio Susillo 41, T665-430375, www.bici4city.com.* Rents bikes and ebikes (€10/20 for 4 hrs, €18/25 for 24 hrs) and audio guides. Also has mountain bikes available and runs guided tours.

Rentabike, *Pl Santa Cruz 4, T955-118228, www.rentabikesevilla.com.* Hires various types of bike (from €20 per day) and also has daily bike tours of the city.

Bullfighting

Although controversial, bullfighting is very popular in Seville; Andalucía is really the cradle of *los toros*. Seville's bullring, **La Maestranza**, is the 2nd most prestigious in Spain and draws top fighters every year. Seville has around 28 *corridas* (bullfights) a season, starting on Easter Sunday, then one every day in Feria, and Thu-Sun until Oct. The highest standard can be seen during the Feria and at the season's end, but you'll pay more for tickets, and they are harder to get hold of. For big fights, it's worth reserving several days in advance at the *taquilla* at the bullring, or book at www. taquillatoros.com.

Football

Seville's main sporting passion is football. While international matches, when they come to town, are mostly played at the Estadio La Cartuja (formerly Estadio Olímpico), the city's clubs, **Real Betis** and **Sevilla**, have their own stadiums. Betis's stadium is being extended (till 2028) and home games are being played at Estadio La Cartuja in the meantime; Sevilla FC will also use the Estadio while its ground is closed for building works in 2027-2029. Going to a match can be a great experience: there's much more of a family atmosphere than in the majority of European countries. One of the 2 teams will be at home almost every weekend of the Spanish season. Games take place mostly on Sat with a few on Mon, Wed and Sun (Sevilla) and on Thu and Sun (Betis). You can buy tickets at the grounds during business hours or before the match; they don't sell out unless they're playing Real Madrid, Barcelona or the volatile local derby.

Tickets are pricey, with the cheapest seats starting at about €25.

Real Betis Balompié, *Estadio Benito Villamarín, Av de la Heliópolis s/n, T954-610340, www.realbetisbalompie.es.* Traditionally representing the working class of the city, Betis play in green-and-white stripes. They have won the league once and the Copa del Rey 3 times.

Sevilla FC, *Estadio Sánchez Pizjuan, Av Eduardo Dato s/n, T954-535353, www.sevillafc.es.* Play in white and red; have also won the league once, and the Europea League 7 times. In the 2010s and early 2020s they were consistently one of the best teams outside of Real Madrid and Barcelona.

Tours

There are several hop-on hop-off **open-top bus tours** of the city, with the usual multilingual commentary. All leave from the Torre del Oro every 30 mins from 1000. They have the same 14 stops and cost €26/27 for a 24-hr ticket, but it's worth checking for special promos.

For a cruise on the river, **Cruceros Turísticos Torre del Oro**, T954-561692, www.crucerostorredeloro.com, departs every 30 mins from 1100 to 2200 (1900 in winter) from the quay by the Torre del Oro. It goes up and down the river, with a commentary pointing out the sights, including the old quays from where Magellan and others once set sail. Bar on board. €17, under-6s free, cruise lasts 1 hr. For a much more intimate experience, **Guadaluxe**, T661-278826, www.guadaluxe.com, offer personal cruises in smaller, solar-powered electric boats, with a friendly skipper and plentiful information on both sights and river wildlife.

There is an extraordinary range of **walking tours** of Seville; contact the tourist information office for details. There are tapas tours, tours on bikes, walks in Triana, and a whole host of themed tours (with more increasingly in English), as well as the standard guided visits to the cathedral and Alcázar. Try **Sevilla Walking Tours**, www.sevillawalkingtours.com.

Watersports

Paddle Surf Sevilla, *C Betis 19, T611-403032, www.paddlesurfsevilla.com*. Rent a paddleboard or kayak on the river, with or without a guide. Also e-foil classes.

Transport

Air

Seville's airport (www.aena.es) is 10 km northeast of the centre. An airport bus service (EA) runs to central Seville (Plaza de Armas bus station) via the main train station. It runs every 10-15 mins, apart from early morning and at night, and takes 35 mins (€5). A taxi to town costs a fixed €25.72 during the day, slightly more at night or weekends.

Easyjet and **Ryanair** connect Seville with several European cities including **London**, and there are many domestic routes run by **Iberia**, **Vueling** and others. For airport information, T954-449000.

Bus

The city of Seville is one of Spain's major destinations for interurban buses. They arrive at 2 stations, Plaza de Armas for destinations north and west, and Prado de San Sebastián for the south and east.

Local Seville's **TUSSAM** buses (T954-010010, www.tussam.es) provide a good service around the city. A single fare is €1.40 (drivers will give change up to a point; you can also pay with contactless), but you can buy a 1- or 3-day tourist card for €5/10 respectively. The most useful bus services are the circular routes: microbus C5 does a tight circuit of the historic centre; buses C1 and C2 run via Santa Justa train station and the Expo site (C1 goes clockwise, C2 anti-clockwise); while C3 (clockwise) and C4 (anti-clockwise) follow the perimeter of the old walls, except for C3's brief detour into Triana. You can examine routes online, download a route map or the TUSSAM app, or pick up a map from the **TUSSAM** office at the Prado de San Sebastián.

Long distance Seville has 2 principal bus stations. The larger, **Plaza de Armas,** by the river near the Puente del Cachorro, T955-038665, www.autobusesplazadearmas.es, serves destinations to the north and west of the city. These include **Madrid** (6.5 hrs, 4 daily), **Huelva** (1 hr 10 mins, 9 daily) and 2 daily buses to **Asturias** via **Mérida** and **Cáceres** (these 2 are also serviced 3 times daily), **Salamanca**, **Zamora** and **León**. There are 6 services to **Lisbon** (6-8 hrs; remember that Portugal is 1 hr behind), and daily buses to **Faro** and **Lagos** in the Algarve. There are also buses to **Alicante**, **Valencia** and **Barcelona**.

The other bus station, **Prado de San Sebastián**, is near the Barrio Santa Cruz on Plaza San Sebastián, T954-417111. It serves destinations east and south of the city. There are frequent buses to **Jerez**

de la Frontera and **Cádiz** (1 hr 30 mins), **Córdoba** (1 hr 45 mins), **Granada** (7 daily, 3 hrs), **Jaén** and **Almería**. There are also connections to a number of smaller Andalucian towns.

For both bus stations, the biggest operators are **Alsa** (www.alsa.es) and **Damas** (www.damas-sa.es).

Car

Seville isn't a great place to have a car due to the narrow one-way streets of the old town and lack of parking. There are plenty of underground car parks that cost about €3 per hr/€25 per day, and many hotels have a car park or access to one.

Car hire There are major international firms at the airport, including **Budget**, T902-110264, www.budget.com, and **Hertz**, T954-514720, www.hertz.com. **Avis**, T954-537861, www.avis.com, and others have offices at the train station, while some car-rental companies are also at Torre Sevilla. Find cheap deals at clickrent.es.

Electric moped hire

You can rent via apps like Acciona ⓘ http://movilidad.acciona.com and Yego ⓘ http://rideyego.com from €0.33/min with the first 15-20 mins free.

Taxis

A ride right across town, for example from the cathedral to the Arco de Macarena, or Triana to the train station, will cost €6-10. Prices rise slightly after 2200, at weekends and during fiestas such as Semana Santa or the Feria. T954-622222 or T954-580000 to book; alternatively use Uber or Cabify.

Train

Seville's modern train station, Santa Justa, is a 15-min walk from the centre on Av Kansas City.

For train information, **Renfe** has a good telephone information line, T912-320320, and its website is www.renfe.com. There's a booking agent in the centre at C Zaragoza 29.

Seville is served by the high-speed AVE train, which cuts travel time to Madrid, Málaga and Córdoba to impressively low levels. It's expensive, so also look at Avlo, Ouigo and Iryo; compare prices on omio.com. If you travel *preferente* class, up to 50% more expensive, you get access to an a/c hospitality waiting room (free food and drinks). Groups can get a great deal booking a table for four in *preferente* class.

There are 10-15 daily trains to **Cádiz** (1 hr 45 mins-2 hrs), stopping at **Jerez** (1 hr). There are 3 daily trains to **Barcelona** (5 fast, 5½ hrs, 1 slow, 12 hrs), 9 to **Valencia** (6 hrs) and lots of high-speed services to **Madrid** (up to 25 high-speed trains daily, 2 hrs 25 mins). To **Córdoba**, there are 11 normal trains daily, 1 hr 30 mins-2 hrs; and up to 35 high-speed trains, 41 mins.

Both fast and slow trains head for **Málaga** (2 hrs/3 hrs 20 mins). There are also trains to **Jaén**, **Huelva** and **Granada**.

Around
Seville city

The bulk of Seville province is undulating farmland, and there's not a great deal of scenic interest. However, north from Seville are the low hills of the Sierra Morena, with lightly forested slopes and valleys making this a great walking destination.

A few small towns beckon through the heat haze east of Seville: Carmona with its excellent Roman graveyard, the spires of Écija, and the elegant ducal seat of Osuna.

★ Sierra Morena

gently rolling countryside, quiet and attractive towns and good walks

North of Seville, the Sierra Morena is a popular weekend trip from the capital. The region's main town is Cazalla de la Sierra, while nearby Constantina is the base for visiting the Parque Natural Sierra Norte, covering much of this part of the province. Heading west, you can cross into the fascinating Huelvan section of the Sierra Morena, home to Spain's finest ham.

Cazalla de la Sierra

This pleasing whitewashed town is the most useful base for exploring the northern reaches of Seville's province. Once an Iberian settlement, it was controlled in turn by the Romans and the Moors, who named it thus (meaning fortified town). The town is now known for its production of *aguardiente*, including the much-imbibed *Miura* cherry-flavoured anis.

The town's church, **Nuestra Señora de la Consolación**, is worth a look. Massive in scale, it's a real mixture of styles, with a keep-like main section featuring layered brick and stone walls; this is *mudéjar* and dates from the 14th-15th century, as does the bell-tower. Other parts were added in the 18th century. Inside, the chancel has elaborate late Gothic vaulting. The ornate *retablo* is a fine 17th-century work, and look out for the beautiful 14th-century baptismal font still in use. Also worth visiting is the **Monasterio La Cartuja** ⓘ *www.lacartujadecazalla.com*, a 15th-century monastery that hosts retreats, astrogazing and other events and activities.

The town has a **tourist office** ⓘ *Plaza Doctor Nosea 1, T954-883562, www.*

Getting around

It's easy to get out of Seville by bus to the main towns listed in the text, although travelling by car would give you more freedom. There are trains from Seville to Cazalla de la Sierra in the Sierra Morena but Cazalla-Constantina train station is 7 km away from the town, so is not very convenient. Buses leave Seville from Plaza de Armas or from La Macarena.

When to go

The best time to visit is spring or autumn, because July and August are baking hot, although temperatures in the Sierra Morena are a bit cooler than elsewhere in Seville province due to the higher altitude.

Time required

Allow at least a day in the Sierra Morena, and a few days for towns east of Seville.

cazalla.org, *Tue-Sun 0900-1400*, with limited material on the area.

There are several marked **walking trails** in the Cazalla area. One of the best is Sendero Las Laderas, which begins from the bottom of the street that runs through the Plaza Mayor past the old town hall. It heads down to the river Huéznar and doubles back through woodland to the town; it takes 1½ hours, but you can extend the walk or even follow the river down to **El Pedroso**, a livestock town with a good hotel; see Where to stay, below. Visit the tourist office for maps.

Constantina

This town, said to be named after the emperor Constantine, is a likeable village topped by a medieval castle with Moorish origins. In the narrow streets of the *morería* below are several fine mansions, while the parish church of Santa María de la Encarnación has a *mudéjar* tower and a Plateresque doorway. The town is the main centre for the Sierra del Norte natural park, which covers some 1650 sq km of the Sierra Morena. It's home to several species of raptor, as well as otters and wild boar. There's a visitor information centre, **El Robledo** ⓘ *T676-073714, Tue-Sun 1000-1400*, on the western edge of town. The office has leaflets on the local marked walking trails, and in autumn runs guided walks that focus on the astonishing variety of wild mushrooms in the area.

Listings Sierra Morena

Where to stay

Cazalla de la Sierra

€€ La Posada del Moro
Paseo del Moro s/n, T954-884858, www.laposadadelmoro.com.
This excellent and welcoming hotel is in Cazalla itself and offers remarkably good value. It's got much rural elegance,

with the emphasis on comfort, and has a pool, pretty garden, and a restaurant that will tempt you to prolong your stay.

€€ Las Navezuelas
Ctra Cazalla–El Robledo s/n, T954-884764, www.lasnavezuelas.com.
Another charming rural establishment, set in a whitewashed *cortijo* with a restored

olive mill and good pool. There are 6 appealing rustic rooms and a variety of self-contained cottages. The price includes breakfast, and the owners can advise on walks in the area and arrange horse riding.

Constantina

€€ Casa Grande

Carretera Cazalla Km 1, A-455, T645-493443, www.casagrandeconstantina.es. Charming small rural hotel with 6 colourful rooms, a pleasant garden and pool overlooking olive-tree-dotted hillsides.

Transport

Cazalla de la Sierra

Cercanía trains run 2 times daily from **Seville** (1 hr 35 mins) via **El Pedroso**, but the station is 7 km from town on the road to Constantina; taxis meet the train. There are also 2-3 buses daily (1 hr 40 mins), which are more convenient.

Constantina

Several daily buses run from Constantina to **Seville** (1 hr).

★ Carmona

sun-baked, sleepy agricultural town

The town of Carmona, encircled by formidable defensive walls, is an easy day trip from Seville, only 36 km east of the city, but couldn't have a more different feel. Outside the old town is one of Andalucía's most interesting archaeological sites, an excavated Roman cemetery. Carmona also offers a couple of excellent luxury hotels in the old town; see Where to stay, below, for details.

Alcázar Puerta de Sevilla

Plaza Blas Infante, T954-190955, http://alcazardelapuertadesevillacarmona.wordpress.com. Mon-Sat 1000-1800, Sun 1000-1500; Jul-Aug Mon-Fri 0900-1500, Sat-Sun 1000-1500. €2, free Mon.

On arrival in Carmona, you'll immediately be struck by the bulky complex of the lower *alcázar*, looming over the narrow entrance gate known as the Puerta de Sevilla. Fortified by successive conquering powers from the Phoenicians to the Castillians, the fortress preserves structures and foundations from all these periods. After an audiovisual presentation, you can wander around the building, which sometimes has temporary exhibitions in one of its halls. There's an informative brochure that helps you pick out the different building stages of the walls. From the top there are worthwhile views over the town and the fertile plains below. The **tourist office** ⓘ *T954-190955, Mon-Sat 1000-1800, Sun 1000-1500, www.turismo.carmona.org*, is located in the Puerta de Sevilla. They can provide a town map and other information.

From here you should wander up through the whitewashed old town, peering into corners. Within this walled area are several churches: Santa María la Mayor preserves the former mosque's Patio de Naranjos and has a good 16th-century *retablo*, while San Pedro has an attractive *mudéjar* tower. Behind Santa María is a

Haciendas

Much of Seville province is taken up by huge farms that produce vast quantities of citrus fruit, olives, wheat, sunflowers and fighting bulls. They are privately owned; this *latifundia* system derives from the days of the Christian Reconquest, when vast parcels of land won from the Moors in battle were distributed among the military leaders. These divisions are still in place and mean that in general local workers can't own their own land but must work as seasonal *jornaleros* on the *haciendas*. The system has contributed to large-scale social inequality in Andalucía and produced much rural unrest, not least in the years leading up to the Spanish Civil War.

The centrepiece of a *hacienda* is the farmhouse, or *cortijo*, which is usually a grand affair, a complex of elegant whitewashed buildings that often includes a chapel. Many *haciendas* offer accommodation that is very luxurious. They are also popular venues for weddings and other celebrations.

For a full list, contact the Seville tourist office, see page 39. Some of the best are:

El Esparragal, T955-782702, www.cortijoelesparragal.es. Famous and fabulous hacienda in grassy grounds 23 km north of Seville in Gerena. Top restaurant and stylish fittings.

Hacienda San Rafael, T955-227116, www.haciendadesanrafael.com. Run by same owners as the Corral del Rey in Seville (see page 40). Lovely, with flowering plants, spacious rooms, and several pools. South of Seville, halfway to Jerez.

---

small archaeological and historical museum. The town centres on the shady Plaza de San Fernando; nearby the Ayuntamiento has a well-crafted Roman mosaic of Medusa in its central courtyard. It's also worth seeking out Plaza de Abastos, an attractive hidden space dedicated to the morning food market.

Roman Necropolis

Avenida Jorge Bonsor 9, T600-143632, www.museosdeandalucia.es/web/conjunto arqueologicodecarmona. Mon-Sat 0900-1800, Sun 0900-1500. Free entry, with audio guide included.

Walking down the hill from the Puerta de Sevilla, you'll come to a long square, Paseo del Estatuto (where the bus from Seville stops). At the far end of this, take the middle of the three streets, which will bring you to this very rewarding site. A series of interesting tombs have been excavated; belonging to wealthy citizens, they were dug into the rock and crowned with marble or stone structures (none of which survive). You can make your way down into many of them, including the massive Tomb of Servilia, daughter of the local governor, where fragments of wall paintings are conserved. Information is in Spanish and English; try to see the small museum before visiting the site, because it puts the material in context.

Where to stay

€€€€ Parador del Rey Don Pedro
C Los Alcázares s/n, T954-141010,
www.parador.es.
The upper Alcázar, once used as a
palace by the charismatic Pedro I, has
been partially restored to house one of
southern Spain's finest paradores. There
are great views over the town and the
plains below. Recommended.

€€€ Alcázar de la Reina
C Hermana Concepción Orellana 2,
T954-196200, www.alcazar-reina.es.
Mudéjar-style hotel on the edge
of the old town – built in 1999, it
looks convincingly older. Rooms are
classically styled. You'll be thankful for
the pool, with its terrace bar, in the
searing summer months; there's also a
restaurant and sauna.

€ Hostal Comercio
C Torre del Oro 56, T954-140018.
Right next to the impressive Puerta
de Sevilla and tucked inside the walls,
this is a spruce option with cordial
management that's good value for
Carmona. It has rooms with or without
bath, as well as a/c (if you thought Seville
was hot, try Carmona).

Restaurants

Dining options centre around Plaza
San Fernando, where there are several
tapas bars. The tourist office has a leaflet
describing a tapas crawl around the town.

€€€ Molino de la Romera
C Puerta de Marchena s/n, T954-142000,
www.molinodelaromera.es.
This restaurant is set in an old olive mill
and serves good local cuisine on its
terrace, which gives views over the plains
below. The wide menu includes cheese
platters, *revueltos*, charcoal-grilled meat,
and game dishes.

Transport

Buses run hourly on the hour weekdays
and a little less often at weekends from the
Prado de San Sebastián station in **Seville**,
50 mins. These drop you off and leave
from the Paseo del Estatuto, just downhill
from the Puerta de Sevilla. From the pretty
Alameda nearby, there are a couple of
daily buses to **Écija** and **Córdoba**.

Écija

baroque churches and abundant *palacios*

Halfway between Seville and Córdoba, this place shouldn't be missed by
those with a liking for Baroque architecture, although try to get here early
because the town is famous for its fearsome summer heat. Once an important
Roman olive oil town named Astigi, it enjoyed great prosperity from the 16th
to 18th centuries as the vast *latifundias* claimed in the Reconquest began to
pay dividends to their inheritors, if not to the landless labourers that sweated
to cultivate them. This wealth is reflected the town's attractive *palacios*. Écija
is also notable for its 18th-century church towers, built after the 1755 Lisbon
earthquake toppled the existing steeples.

Located in the centre of town is a **tourist office** ⓘ *C Elvira 1, T955-902933, www.turismoecija.com, Mon-Sat 1000-1400, 1630-1830 Sun 1000-1400 (Jul to mid-Sep 1000-1400)*, with plenty to offer; the website is also good.

The grandest of Écija's palaces is the **Palacio de Peñaflor** ⓘ *C Emilio Castelar 26, www.turismoecija.com, Mon 1000-1330, 1630-1830, Sat 1000-1400, 1730-2000, Sun 1100-1400, €3 including audio guide*. The curved exterior is striking; it's known locally as the house of the long balcony, this feature being nearly 60 m long. The façade is decorated with frescoes, while inside is a fine staircase topped by a cupola with extravagantly decorative stucco work. The central patio has a marble fountain and a colourful dado of agate and different hues of marble.

Another stately residence near the Plaza de España is **Palacio de Benameji** ⓘ *Plaza de la Constitución, www.museo.ecija.es, Jun-Sep Tue-Fri 1000-1430, Sat 1000-1400, 2000-2200, Sun 1000-1500; Oct-May Tue-Fri 1000-1330, 1630-1830, Sat 1000-1400, 1730-2000, Sun 1000-1500; €4 including audio guide*, which has been converted into a beautiful museum displaying Tartessian and Roman finds, as well as some exhibits on local culture, particularly horse breeding.

The churches are too plentiful to list in detail here, but you'll come across nearly all of them by strolling in the area around Plaza de España. Most of the towers are cheerfully coloured in bright yellow and blue ceramic tiles.

Listings Écija

Where to stay

Écija's accommodation options are limited.

€ Hotel Platería
C Platería 1, T955-902754, www.hotelplateria.net.
Tucked away down a side road, the hospitable Platería has well-furnished modern rooms set around a central atrium. There's also an excellent low-priced restaurant. An all-round bargain.

Restaurants

€€ Las Ninfas Gastrobar
C Elvira 1, T955-897485, www.lasninfas.com.
This stylish restaurant occupying part of the same *palacio* as the museum is decorated with various objets d'art and offers well-prepared local cuisine, including some excellent steaks, as well as a magnificent patio.

Festivals

Sep The town's **feria** takes place for 6 days in the 2nd week of the month. There's also a *cante jondo* **flamenco festival** night, which attracts excellent performers.

Transport

Bus
There are 10 weekday buses (4-5 at weekends) to and from Prado San Sebastián station in **Seville** (1 hr 15 mins). There are also 4 daily buses that run to **Córdoba** and a few to **Carmona** and **Osuna**.

South of Écija, this little-visited ducal town owes most of its monuments to the wealthy Girón family, who have held the title since the 16th century. Osuna had been an important Iberian and then Roman town (Urso).

In the 18th-century Museo de Osuna stands the **tourist office** ⓘ *C Sevilla 37, T954-815732, www.osuna.es, mid-Jun to mid-Sep Tue-Sun 0930-1430; mid-Sep to mid-Jun Tue-Sat 1000-1400, 1700-2000, Sun 1000-1400.*

The town is situated on a steep hill, the top of which is dominated by two buildings, the collegiate church and the old university. **Santa María de la Asunción** ⓘ *www.colegiatadeosuna.es, admission by guided tour Tue-Sun 1015-1315, 1600-1700 (0915-1315 summer), €6,* was founded in the mid-16th century by Juan Téllez Girón, who spared no expense in the construction. It's a beautifully proportioned Renaissance building (although there are later additions) in creamy stone. The interior is harmoniously arched and has a series of excellent paintings by Ribera, including a Crucifixion and a harried-looking San Jerónimo in the sacristy. The pantheon of the Dukes of Osuna is an atmospheric and highly ornamented Plateresque crypt.

The university stands behind the church and has a fine patio with a pure Renaissance simplicity to it. Further up the hill is **El Coto de Las Canteras** ⓘ *http://elcotolascanteras.com, Mon-Sun 1000-1400, Sat also 1600-1900, €4.* This ancient sandstone quarry with magnificent Turdetanian-style (new) carved façade has been converted into a 1,400-seater auditorium which hosts concerts.

In the town below, there are several other churches worth visiting, including the Iglesia de la Merced, which has a barrel-vaulted ceiling.

Listings Osuna

Where to stay

€€ Palacio Marqués de la Gomera
C San Pedro 20, T954-812632,
www.hotelpalaciodelmarques.es.
Where else would you want to stay in Osuna other than a palace? This place fits the bill perfectly, set around a round-arched patio. The 18th-century building is furnished in period style. Rooms on the upper level are more attractive (and pricier) with wooden ceilings, but all are spacious and good value. The hotel also has 2 restaurants and a small garden.

Transport

Bus
There are 6 daily buses to Osuna from **Seville**'s Prado de San Sebastián bus station. There are also buses to **Écija**, **Antequera** and a couple on to **Málaga** itself.

Background
Andalucía

History

Spain's proximity to Africa meant that Andalucía was one of Europe's front lines for migrating hominids from the south. Discoveries near Burgos, in Spain's north, attest that prehistoric humans inhabited the peninsula 1.3 million years ago; these are the oldest known hominid remains in western Europe. Andalucía was a likely entry point.

Around the turn of the first millennium, the face of the region was changing significantly. The people named as **Iberians** in later texts, and probably of local origin, inhabited the area and were joined by some **Celts**, although these peoples predominantly settled in the north of the peninsula. The Iberians had two distinct languages, unrelated to the Indo-European family, and benefited significantly from the arrival of another group, the **Phoenicians**.

These master sailors and merchants from the Levant set up many trading stations on the Andalucian coast. The Phoenicians set about trading with the Iberians, and began extensive mining operations, extracting gold, silver and copper from Andalucía's richly endowed soils.

Profitable contact with this maritime superpower led to the emergence of the wealthy local **Tartessian civilisation**. Famed in classical sources as a mystical region where demigods walked streets paved with gold, precious little is actually known about this culture. Although they developed writing, it is undeciphered. While it seems that they had an efficiently controlled society, no site worthy of being identified as the capital, Tartessos, has been excavated. Seemingly based in the region around the Guadalquivir valley, including Carmona, the Tartessians were highly skilled craftsmen; the Carambolo hoard found in Seville province consists of astonishingly intricate and beautiful gold jewellery.

Towards the end of the sixth century BC, the Tartessian culture seems to disappear and Iberian settlements appear to have reverted to self-governing towns, usually fortified places on hilltops.

As Phoenician power waned, their heirs and descendants, the **Carthaginians**, increased their operations in the western Mediterranean and settled throughout Andalucía. While the Phoenicians had enjoyed a mostly prosperous and peaceful relationship with the local peoples, the Carthaginians were more concerned with conquest and, under **Hamilcar Barca** and his relatives **Hasdrubal** and **Hannibal**, they took control of much of southern Spain and increased mining operations. The Iberian tribes, who included the **Turdetanians**, the group that had inherited the Tartessian mantle in the Guadalquivir basin, seem to have had mixed relations with the Barcid rulers. Some towns accepted Carthaginian control, while others resisted it.

Hispania

The Romans were bent on ending Punic power in the Mediterranean and soon realised that the peninsula was rapidly becoming a second Carthage. Roman troops arrived in Spain in 218 BC and Andalucía became one of the major theatres of the Second Punic War. Some of the local tribes, such as the Turdetanians, sided with the Romans against the Carthaginians and the final Roman victory came in 206 BC, at the Battle of Ilipa near Seville. The Carthaginians were kicked out of the peninsula.

During the war, the Romans had established the city of Itálica near Seville as a rest camp for dissatisfied Italian troops but it was only some time after the end of hostilities that the Romans appear to have developed an interest in the peninsula itself. Realising the vast resources of the region, they set about conquering the whole of Hispania, a feat that they did not accomplish until late in the first century BC. It was the Romans who first created the idea of Spain as a single geographical entity, a concept it has struggled with ever since.

The wealth of Hispania meant that it became an important pawn in the power struggles of the Roman republic and it was in Andalucía, near modern Bailén, that **Julius Caesar** finally defeated Pompey's forces in 45 BC. With peace established, Caesar set about establishing colonies in earnest; many of Andalucía's towns and cities were built or rebuilt by the Romans in this period. Caesar knew the region pretty well; he had campaigned here in 68 BC and later had been governor of Hispania Ulterior. The contacts he had made during this period served him well and Caesar rewarded the towns that had helped him against Pompey, such as Seville, by conferring full Roman citizenship on the inhabitants. Later, Vespasian granted these rights to the whole of the peninsula.

Augustus redivided Hispania into three provinces; the southernmost, **Baetica**, roughly corresponded to modern Andalucía. Initially administered from Córdoba, the capital was switched to Hispalis (Seville), which, along with neighbouring Itálica, prospered under the Imperial regime. The south of Spain became a real Roman heartland, the most Roman of the Roman colonies. Itálica was the birthplace of the Emperor Trajan and sometime home of his protégé Hadrian. The first century AD was a time of much peace and prosperity and Andalucía's grandest Roman remains date largely from this period.

It was probably during this century that the bustling Andalucian ports heard their first whisperings of Christianity, which arrived early in the peninsula. Around this time, too, a Jewish population began to build up – the beginnings of what was a crucial segment of Andalucian society for 1500 years.

A gradual decline began late in the second century AD, with raids from North Africa nibbling at the edges of a weakening empire. Christianity had become a dominant force, but religious squabblings exacerbated rather than eased the tension.

In the fifth century, as the Roman order tottered, various barbarian groups streamed across the Pyrenees and created havoc. **Alans** and **Vandals** established themselves in the south of Spain; it has been (almost certainly erroneously) suggested that the latter group lent their name to Andalucía. The Romans enlisted the Visigoths to restore order on their behalf. This they succeeded in doing, but they liked the look of the land and returned for good after they lost control of their French territories. After a period of much destruction and chaos, a fairly tenuous Visigothic control ensued. They used Seville as an early capital, but later transferred their seat of power to Toledo.

The Visigoths

While there is little enough archaeological and historical evidence from this period, what has been found shows that the Visigoths had inherited Roman customs and architecture to a large degree, while many finds exhibit highly sophisticated carving and metalworking techniques. The bishop and writer San Isidoro produced some of Europe's most important post-Roman texts from his base in Seville. There were likely comparatively few Visigoths: a small warrior class ruling with military strength best fits the evidence, and they seem to have fairly rapidly become absorbed into the local culture.

The seventh century saw numerous changes of rulers, many of whom imposed increasingly severe strictures on the substantial Jewish population of the peninsula. Restrictions on owning property, attempted forced conversions and other impositions foreshadowed much later events in Spain. The Visigoths possibly paid a heavy price for this persecution, and several historians opine that the Moorish invasion was substantially aided by the support of Jewish communities that (rightly, as it turned out) viewed the conquerors as liberators.

Al-Andalus

In AD 711 an event occurred that was to define Spanish history for the next eight centuries. The teachings of Muhammad had swept across North Africa and the Moors were to take most of Spain before the prophet had been dead for even a century. After a number of exploratory raids, Tarik, governor of Tanger, crossed the straits with a small force of mostly Berber soldiers. Joined by a larger force under the command of the governor of North Africa, Musa ibn-Nusair, the Moors then defeated and slew the Visigothic king Roderic somewhere near Tarifa. The conquests continued under Musa's son Abd al-Aziz until almost the whole peninsula was in Moorish hands: the conquest had taken less than three years, an extraordinary feat. Soon the Muslim armies were well advanced on the *autoroutes* of southern France.

The Moors named their Iberian dominions Al-Andalus and, while these lands grew and shrank over time, the heartland was always in the south. Romantic depictions of Al-Andalus as a multicultural paradise are not entirely accurate; the situation is best described by Richard Fletcher as one of 'grudging toleration, but toleration nonetheless'. Christians and Jews were allowed relative freedom of worship and examples of persecution are comparatively few. Moorish texts throughout the history of Al-Andalus reveal a condescending attitude towards non-Muslims (and vice versa in Christian parts of Spain), but it is probable that in day-to-day life there was large-scale cultural contact, a process described by Spanish historians as *convivencia* (cohabitation). The conversion of Christians and Jews to Islam was a gradual but constant process; this was no doubt given additional impetus by the fact that Muslims didn't pay any tax beyond the alms required as part of their faith. Christian converts to Islam were known as *muwallads*, while those who remained Christian under the rule of the Moors are called *mozárabes* or Mozarabs.

Arabic rapidly became the major language of southern Spain, even among non-Muslims. The number of Arabic words in modern Spanish attests to this. Many of them refer to agriculture and crops; the Moors brought with them vastly improved farming and irrigation methods, as well as a host of fruits and vegetables not grown before on the peninsula's soil. This, combined with wide and profitable trading routes in the Mediterranean, meant that Al-Andalus began to thrive economically, which must have assisted in the pacification of the region. Córdoba's Mezquita, begun in the eighth century, was expanded and made richer in various phases through this period; this can be seen as reflecting both the growing wealth and the increasing number of worshippers.

Christian kingdoms

Geography divides Spain into distinct regions, which have tended to persist through time, and it was one of these – Asturias – that the Moors had trouble with. They were defeated in what was presumably a minor skirmish in AD 717 at Covadonga, in the far northern mountains. It was hardly a crippling blow to the Moors, but it probably sowed the seeds of what became the **Asturian** and **Leonese** monarchy. They established an organised little kingdom of sorts with a capital that shifted about but settled on Oviedo in AD 808. The Asturian kingdom began to grow in strength and the long process of the *Reconquista*, the Christian reconquest of the peninsula, began. As the Christians moved south, they resettled many towns and villages that had lain in ruins since Roman times.

Both the Christian and Muslim powers were painfully aware of their vulnerability and constructed a series of massive fortresses that faced each other across the central plains. The Muslim fortresses were particularly formidable: high eyries with commanding positions, accurately named the 'front teeth' of Al-Andalus. Relations between Christian and Muslim Spain were curious. While there were frequent campaigns, raids and battles, there was also a high level of peaceful contact and diplomacy.

The caliphate faced a very real threat from the Fatimid dynasty in North Africa and campaigning in the Christian north was one way to fund the fortification of the Mediterranean coast. No-one campaigned more successfully than the formidable Al-Manzur, succeeding in sacking almost every city in northern Spain in a 30-year campaign of terror. Al-Manzur was succeeded by his equally adept son Abd al-Malik, but when he died young in 1008, the caliphate disintegrated with two rival Umayyad claimants seeking to fill the power vacuum.

Twenty years of civil war followed. Both sides employed a variety of Christian and Muslim mercenaries to prosecute their claims to the caliphal throne, and the situation was bloody and chaotic in the extreme. When the latest puppet caliph was deposed in 1031, any pretence of centralised government evaporated and Berber generals, regional administrators and local opportunists seized power in towns across Al-Andalus, forming the small city-states known as the *taifa* kingdoms – *taifa* means faction in Arabic.

This first *taifa* period lasted for most of the rest of the 11th century and in many ways sounded an early death-knell for Muslim Spain. Petty rivalries between the neighbouring *taifas* led to the recruitment of Christian military aid in exchange for large sums of cash. This influx led in turn to the strengthening of the northern kingdoms and many *taifas* were then forced to pay tribute, or protection money, to Christian rulers or face obliteration.

The major *taifas* in Andalucía were Seville and Granada, which gradually swallowed up several of their smaller neighbours. The Abbadid rulers of Seville led a hedonistic life, the kings Al-Mu'tadid and his son Al-Mu'tamid penning poetry between revelries and romantic liaisons.

The Christian north lost little time in taking advantage of the weak *taifa* states. As well as exacting punitive tribute, the Castilian king Alfonso VI had his eye on conquests and crossed far beyond the former front line of the Duero valley. His capture of highly symbolic Toledo, the old Visigothic capital and Christian centre, in 1085, finally set alarm bells ringing in the verse-addled brains of the *taifa* kings.

They realised they needed help, and they called for it across the Straits to Morocco. Since the middle of the 11th century, a group of tribesmen known as the **Almoravids** had been establishing control there and their leader, Yusuf, was invited across to Al-Andalus to help combat Alfonso VI. A more unlikely alliance is hard to imagine: the Almoravids were barely literate desert warriors with a strong and fundamentalist Islamic faith, a complete contrast to the *taifa* rulers in their blossom-scented pleasure domes. The Almoravid armies defeated Alfonso near Badajoz in 1086 but were appalled at the state of Islam in Al-Andalus, so Yusuf decided to stay and establish a stricter observance. He rapidly destroyed the *taifa* system and established governors, answerable to Marrakech, in the major towns, including Seville, having whisked the poet-king off to wistful confinement in Fez.

Almoravid rule was marked by a more aggressive approach to the Christian north, which was matched by the other side. Any hope of retaking much territory soon subsided, as rebellions from the local Andalusi and pressure from another dynasty, the Almohads in Morocco, soon took their toll. This was compounded by another factor: tempted no doubt by worldly pleasures and free-poured spirits, the hard-line Almoravids were lapsing into softer ways. Control again dissolved into local *taifas*.

The Almohads, who by now controlled Morocco, began crossing the Straits to intervene in Andalusi military affairs. Although similarly named and equally hard line in their Islamism, the Almohads were significantly different from the Almoravids, with a canny grasp of politics and advanced military tactics. They gained control over the whole of what is now Andalucía by about 1172. Much surviving military architecture in Andalucía was built by the Almohads, including the great walls and towers of Seville. Yet they too lapsed into decadence, and bungled planning led to the very costly military defeat at Las Navas de Tolosa at the hands of Alfonso VIII in 1212. This was a major blow. Alfonso's son Fernando III (1217-1252) capitalised on his father's success, taking Córdoba in 1236, Jaén, the 'Iron Gate' of Andalucía, in 1246, and then Seville, the Almohad capital, in 1248, after a two-year siege. The loss of the most important city of Al-Andalus, mourned across the Muslim world, was effectively the end of Moorish power in Spain, although the emirate of Granada lingered on for another 250 years. Fernando, sainted for his efforts, expelled all Seville's Moorish inhabitants, setting a pattern of intolerance towards the *mudéjares*, the Muslims who lived under Christian rule.

What was left of Muslim Spain was the emirate of Granada. The nobleman Muhammad Ibn-Yusuf Ibn-Nasr set himself up here as ruler in 1237 and gave his name to the Nasrid dynasty. He sent a detachment of troops to help besiege Seville, a humiliation that eloquently shows how little real power he had.

Meanwhile, the Christians were consolidating their hold on most of Andalucía, building churches and cathedrals over the mosques they encountered and trying to find settlers to work the vast new lands at their disposal because many of the Moors had fled to the kingdom of Granada or across the sea to North Africa. Nobles involved in the *Reconquista* claimed vast tracts of territory, estates known as *latifundias* that still exist today and that have been the cause of numerous social problems in Andalucía over the centuries.

The Nasrid kingdom continued to survive, partly because its boundaries were extremely well fortified with thousands of defensive towers. In the second half of the 14th century the enlightened Castilian king Pedro I was employing Moorish craftsmen to recreate Seville's Alcázar in sumptuous style.

The Golden Age

In the 15th century, there were regular rebellions and much kinstrife over succession in the Nasrid kingdom, which was beginning to seem ripe for the plucking. One of the reasons this hadn't yet happened was that the Christian kingdoms were involved in similar succession disputes. Then, in 1469, an event occurred that was to spell the end for the Moorish kingdom and have a massive impact on the history of the world. The heir to the Aragonese throne, Fernando, married Isabel, heiress of Castilla, in a secret ceremony in Valladolid. The implications were enormous. Aragón was still a power in the Mediterranean (Fernando was also king of Sicily) and Castilla's domain covered much of the peninsula. The unification under the Reyes Católicos, as the monarchs became known, marked the beginnings of Spain as we know it today. There were plenty of opponents to the union, however, and forces in support of Juana, Isabel's elder (but claimed by her to be illegitimate) sister waged wars across Castilla.

When the north was once more at peace, the monarchs found that they ruled the entire peninsula except for Portugal, with which a peace had just been negotiated, the small mountain kingdom of Navarra, which Fernando stood a decent chance of inheriting at some stage anyway, and the decidedly un-Catholic Nasrids in their sumptuous southern palaces. The writing was on the wall and Fernando and Isabel began their campaign. Taking Málaga in 1487 and Almería in 1489, they were soon at Granada's gates. The end came with a whimper when King Boabdil surrendered the keys of the great city on New Year's Day in 1492.

The Catholic Monarchs had put an end to Al-Andalus, which had endured in various forms for the best part of 800 years. They celebrated in true Christian style by kicking the Jews out of Spain. Andalucía's Jewish population had been hugely significant for a millennium and a half, heavily involved in commerce, shipping and literature throughout the peninsula. But hatred of them had begun to grow in the 14th century and there had been many pogroms, including an especially vicious one in 1391, which began in Seville and spread to most other cities in Christian Spain. Many converted during these years to escape the murderous atmosphere, and they became known as *conversos*. The decision to expel those who hadn't converted was far more that of the pious Isabel than the pragmatic Fernando, and has to be seen in the light of the paranoid Christianising climate. The Jews were given four months to leave the kingdom, and even the *conversos* soon found themselves under the iron hammer of the Inquisition.

In 1492 Cristóbal Colón (Christopher Columbus) had been petitioning the royal couple for ships and funds to mount an expedition to sail westwards to the Indies. Finally granted his request, he set off from Palos de la Frontera near Huelva and, after a deal of hardship, reached what he thought was his goal. In the wake of Columbus's discovery, the treaty of Tordesillas in 1494 partitioned the Atlantic between Spain and Portugal and led to the era of Spanish colonisation of the Americas. In many ways, this was an extension of the Reconquista as young men hardened on the Castilian and Extremaduran *meseta* crossed the seas with a zeal for conquest, riches and land. Andalucía was both enriched and crippled by this exodus: while the cities flourished on the New World booty and trade, the countryside was denuded of people to work the land. The biggest winner proved to be Seville, which was granted a monopoly over New World trade by the Catholic Monarchs in 1503. It grew rapidly and became one of western Europe's foremost cities. In 1519, another notable endeavour began here. Ferdinand Magellan set sail from Triana, via Sanlúcar de Barrameda, in an attempt to circumnavigate the world. He didn't make it, dying halfway, but one of the expedition's ships did. Skippered by a Basque, Juan Sebastián Elkano, it arrived some three years later.

Isabel died in 1504, but refused to settle her Castilian throne on her husband, Fernando, to his understandable annoyance, because the two had succeeded in uniting virtually the whole of modern Spain under their joint rule. The inheritance passed to their mad daughter, Juana la Loca, and her husband, Felipe of Burgundy (el Hermoso or the Fair), who came to Spain in 1506 to claim their inheritance. Felipe soon died, however, and his wife's obvious inability to govern led to Fernando being recalled as regent of the united Spain until the couple's son, Carlos, came of age. During this period Fernando completed the boundaries of modern Spain by annexing Navarra. On his deathbed he reluctantly agreed to name Carlos heir to Aragón and its territories, thus preserving the unity he and Isabel had forged. Carlos I of Spain (Carlos V) inherited vast tracts of European land: Spain and southern Italy from his maternal grandparents, and Austria, Burgundy and the Low Countries from his paternal ones. He was shortly named Holy Roman Emperor and, if all that worldly power weren't enough, his friend, aide and tutor, Adrian of Utrecht, was soon elected Pope.

The first two Habsburg monarchs, Carlos V and then his son Felipe II, relied on the income from the colonies to pursue wars (often unwillingly) on several European fronts. It couldn't last; Spain's Golden Age has been likened by historian Felipe Fernández-Armesto to a dog walking on its hind legs. While Seville prospered from the American expansion, the provinces declined, hastened by a drain of citizens to the New World. The *comunero* revolt expressed the frustrations of a region that was once the focus of optimistic Christian conquest and agricultural wealth, but had now become peripheral to the designs of a 'foreign' monarchy. Resentment was exacerbated by the fact that the king still found it difficult to extract taxes from the *cortes* of Aragón or Catalunya, so Castilla (of which Andalucía was a part) bankrolled a disproportionate amount of the crippling costs of the running of a worldwide empire. The growing administrative requirements of managing an empire had forced the previously itinerant Castilian monarchs to choose a capital and Felipe II picked the small town of Madrid in 1561, something of a surprise given that Seville or Valladolid were more obvious choices. Although central, Madrid was remote, tucked away behind a shield of hills in the interior. This seemed in keeping with the somewhat paranoid nature of Habsburg rule. And beyond all other things, they were paranoid about threats to the Catholic religion, the biggest of which, of course, they perceived to be Protestantism. This paranoia was costly in the extreme.

Decline of the empire

The struggle of the Spanish monarchy to control the spread of Protestantism was a major factor in the decline of the empire. Felipe II fought expensive and ultimately unwinnable wars in Flanders that bankrupted the state, while within the country the absolute ban on the works of heretical philosophers, scientists and theologists left Spain behind in Renaissance Europe. Felipe II's successors didn't have his strength of character: Felipe III was ineffectual and dominated by his advisers, while Felipe IV, so sensitively portrayed by Velázquez, tried hard but was indecisive and unfortunate. As well as being unwillingly involved in several costly wars overseas, there was also a major rebellion in Catalunya in the mid-17th century. The decline of the monarchy parallelled a physical decline in the monarchs, as the inbred Habsburgs became more and more deformed and weak; the last of them, Carlos II, was a tragic victim of contorted genetics who died childless and plunged the nation into a war of succession.

While the early 17th century saw the zenith of the Seville school of painting, the city was in decline: the expulsion of the *moriscos* had removed a vital labour force, and merchants and bankers were packing up and going elsewhere as the crown's economic problems led to increasingly punitive taxation. The century saw several plagues in Andalucian cities, and Seville lost an incredible half of its inhabitants in 1649.

The death of poor heirless Carlos II was a long time coming and foreign powers were circling to try to secure a favourable succession to the throne of Spain. Carlos eventually named the French duke Felipe de Bourbon as his successor, much to the concern of England and Holland, who declared war on France. War broke out throughout Spain until the conflict's eventual resolution at the Treaty of Utrecht, at which Britain received Gibraltar, and Spain also lost its Italian and Low Country possessions.

The Bourbon dynasty succeeded in bringing back a measure of stability and wealth to Spain in the 18th century. Seville's decline and the silting up of the Guadalquivir led to the monarchs establishing the port of Cádiz as the centre for New World trade in its place and Spain's oldest city prospered again.

The 19th century in Andalucía and Spain was turbulent to say the least. The 18th century had ended with a Spanish-French conflict in the wake of the French revolution. Peace was made after two years, but worse was to follow. First was a heavy defeat for a joint Spanish-French navy by Nelson off Cabo Trafalgar near Cádiz. Next Napoleon tricked Carlos IV. Partitioning Portugal between France and Spain seemed like a good idea to Spain, which had always coveted its western neighbour. It wasn't until the French armies seemed more interested in Madrid than Lisbon that Carlos IV got the message. Forced to abdicate in favour of his rebellious son Fernando, he was then summoned to a conference with Bonaparte at Bayonne, with his son, wife and Manuel Godoy, his able and trusted adviser (who is often said to have been loved even more by the queen than the king). Napoleon had his own brother Joseph (known among Spaniards as *Pepe Botellas* for his heavy drinking) installed on the throne.

On 2 May 1808 (still a red-letter day in Spain), the people revolted against this arrogant gesture and Napoleon sent in the troops later that year. Soon after, a hastily assembled Spanish army inflicted a stunning defeat on the French at Bailén, near Jaén; the Spaniards were then joined by British and Portuguese forces and the ensuing few years were known in Spain as the Guerra de Independencia (War of Independence). The allied forces under Wellington won important battles after the initiative had been taken by the French. The behaviour of both sides was brutal both on and off the battlefield. Marshal Soult's long retreat across the region saw him loot town after town; his men robbed tombs and burned priceless archives. The allied forces were little better: the men Wellington had referred to as the 'scum of the earth' sacked the towns they conquered with similar destructiveness.

Significant numbers of Spaniards had been in favour of the French invasion and were opposed to the liberal republican movements that sprang up in its wake. In 1812, a revolutionary council in Cádiz, on the point of falling to the French, drafted a constitution proclaiming a democratic parliamentary monarchy of sorts. Liberals had high hopes that this would be brought into effect at the end of the war, but the returning king, Fernando, revoked it. Meanwhile, Spain was on the point of losing its South American colonies, which were being mobilised under *libertadores* such as Simón Bolívar. Spain sent troops to restore control, a thankless assignment for the soldiers involved. One of the armies was preparing to leave Cádiz in 1820 when the commander, Rafael de Riego, invoked the 1812 constitution and refused to fight under the 'unconstitutional' monarchy. Much of the army joined him and the king was forced to recognise the legality of the constitution. Things soon dissolved though, with the 'liberals' (the first use of the word) being split into factions and opposed by the church and aristocracy. Eventually, King Fernando called on the king of France to send an invading army; the liberals were driven backwards to Seville, then to Cádiz where they were defeated, and Riego was taken to his execution in Madrid. In many ways this conflict mirrored the later Spanish Civil War. Riego, who remained (and remains) a hero of the democratically minded, did not die in vain: his stand impelled much of Europe on the road to constitutional democracy, although it took Spain itself over a century and a half to find that stability.

The remainder of the century was to see clash after clash of liberals against conservatives, progressive cities against reactionary countryside, restrictive centre against outward-looking periphery. Spain finally lost its empire because the strife-torn homeland could do little against the independence movements of Latin America. When Fernando died, another war of succession broke out, this time between supporters of his brother Don Carlos and his infant daughter Isabella. The so-called Carlist Wars of 1833-1839, 1847-1849 (although this is sometimes not counted as one) and 1872-1876 were politically complex. Don Carlos represented conservatism and his support was drawn from a number of sources. Wealthy landowners, the church and the reactionary peasantry, with significant French support, lined up against the loyalist army, the liberals and the urban middle and working classes. In between and during the wars, a series of *pronunciamientos* (coups d'état) plagued the monarchy. In 1834, after Fernando's death, another, far less liberal constitution was drawn up. An important development for Andalucía took place in 1835 when the prime minister, desperate for funds to prosecute the war against the Carlists, confiscated church and monastery property in the Disentailment Act. The resulting sale of the vast estates aided nobody but the large landowners who bought them up at bargain prices, further skewing the distribution of arable land in Andalucía towards the wealthy.

Despite the grinding poverty, the middle years of the 19th century saw the beginnings of what was eventually to save Andalucía: tourism. Travellers, such as Washington Irving, Richard Ford and Prosper Mérimée, came to the region and enthralled the world with tales of sighing Moorish princesses, feisty *sevillanas*, bullfights, gypsies, bandits and passion. While to the 21st-century eye the uncritical romanticism of these accounts is evident, they captured much of the magic that contemporary visitors still find in the region, and have inspired generations of travellers to investigate Spain's south.

During the third Carlist war, the king abdicated and the short-lived First Spanish Republic was proclaimed, ended by a military-led restoration a year later. The Carlists were defeated but remained strong and played a prominent part in the Spanish Civil War. (Indeed, there's still a Carlist party.) As if generations of war weren't enough, the wine industry of Andalucía received a crippling blow with the arrival of the phylloxera pest, which devastated the region.

The 1876 constitution proclaimed by the restored monarchy after the third Carlist war provided for a peaceful alternation of power between liberal and conservative parties. In the wake of decades of strikes and *pronunciamientos* this was not a bad solution and the introduction of the vote for the whole male population in 1892 offered much hope. The ongoing curse, however, was *caciquismo*, a system whereby elections and governments were hopelessly rigged by influential local groups of 'mates'.

Spain lost its last overseas possessions – Cuba, Puerto Rico and the Philippines – in the 'Disaster' of 1898. The introspective turmoil caused by this event gave the name to the '1898 generation', a forward-thinking movement of artists, philosophers and poets among whom were numbered the poets Antonio Machado and Juan Ramón Jiménez, the philosophers José Ortega y Gasset and Miguel de Unamuno, and the painter Ignacio de Zuloaga. It was a time of discontent, with regular strikes culminating in the Semana Trágica (tragic week) in Barcelona in 1909, a week of church-burning and rioting sparked by the government's decision to send a regiment of Catalan conscripts to fight in the 'dirty war' in Morocco; the revolt was then brutally suppressed by the army. The growing disaffectation of farmworkers in Andalucía, forced for centuries into seasonal labour on the vast *latifundias* with no security and minimal earnings, led to a strong anarchist movement in the region. The CNT, the most prominent of the 20th-century anarchist confederations, was founded in Seville in 1910.

The Second Republic, the Civil War and the Dictatorship

The early years of the 20th century saw repeated changes of government under King Alfonso XIII. A massive defeat in Morocco in 1921 increased the discontent with the monarch, but General Miguel Primo de Rivera, a native of Jerez de la Frontera, led a coup and installed himself as dictator under Alfonso in 1923. One of his projects was the grandiose Ibero-American exhibition in Seville. The preparation for this lavish event effectively created the modern city we know today and, despite bankrupting the city, set the framework for a 20th-century urban centre.

Primo de Rivera's rule was relatively benign, but growing discontent eventually forced the king to dismiss him. Having broken his coronation oath to uphold the constitution, Alfonso himself was soon toppled as republicanism swept the country. The anti-royalists achieved excellent results in elections in 1931 and the king drove to Cartagena and took a boat out of the country to exile. The Second Republic was joyfully proclaimed by the left.

Things moved quickly in the short period of the republic. The new leftist government moved fast to drastically reduce the church's power. The haste was ill-advised and triumphalist and served to severely antagonise the conservatives and the military. The granting of home rule to Catalunya was even more of a blow to the establishment and their belief in Spain as an indissoluble *patria*, or fatherland.

Through this period, there was increasing anarchist activity in Andalucía, where land was seized as a reaction to the archaic *latifundia* system under which prospects for the workers, who were virtually serfs, were nil. Anarchist co-operatives were formed to share labour and produce in many of the region's rural areas. Squabbling among leftist factions contributed to the government's lack of control of the country, which propelled the right to substantial gains in elections in 1933. Government was eventually formed by a centrist coalition, with the right powerful enough to heavily influence lawmaking. The 1933 elections also saw José Antonio Primo de Rivera, son of the old dictator, elected to a seat on a fascist platform. Although an idealist, he founded the Falange, a group of fascist youth that became an increasingly powerful force and one which was responsible for some of the most brutal deeds before, during and immediately after the Spanish Civil War.

The new government set about reversing the reforms of its predecessors; provocative and illegal infractions of labour laws by employers didn't help the workers' moods. Independence rumblings in Catalunya and the Basque country began to gather momentum, but it was in Asturias that the major confrontation took place. The left, mainly consisting of armed miners, seized the civil buildings of the province and the government response was harsh, with generals Goded and Franco embarking on a brutal spree of retribution with their well-trained Moroccan troops.

The left was outraged and the right feared complete revolution; the centre ceased to exist, as citizens and politicians were forced to one side or the other. The elections of February 1936 were very close, but the left unexpectedly defeated the right. In an increasingly violent climate, mobilised Socialist youth and the Falange were clashing daily, while land seizures continued. A group of generals began to plan a coup and in July 1936 a military conspiracy saw garrisons throughout Spain rise against the government and try to seize control of their provinces and towns. Within a few days, battle lines were clearly drawn between the Republicans (government) and the Nationalists, a coalition of military, Carlists, fascists and the Christian right. Most of northern Spain rapidly went under Nationalist control, while Madrid remained Republican. In Andalucía, Córdoba, Cádiz, Seville, Huelva and Granada were taken by Nationalists, but the remainder was in loyalist hands.

In the immediate aftermath of the uprising, frightening numbers of civilians were shot behind the lines, including the Granadan poet, Federico García Lorca. This brutality continued throughout the war, with chilling atrocities committed on both sides.

The most crucial blow of the war was struck early. Francisco Franco, one of the army's best generals, had been posted to the Canary Islands by the government, who were rightly fearful of coup attempts. As the uprising occurred, Franco was flown to Morocco where he took command of the crack North African legions. The difficulty was crossing into Spain: this was achieved in August in an airlift across the Straits of Gibraltar by German planes. Franco swiftly advanced through Andalucía where his battle-hardened troops met with little resistance. Meanwhile, the other main battle lines were north of Madrid and in Aragón, where the Republicans made a determined early push for Zaragoza.

At a meeting of the revolutionary generals in October 1936, Franco had himself declared *generalísimo*, the supreme commander of the Nationalists. Few could have suspected that he would rule the nation for nearly four decades. Although he had conquered swathes of Andalucía and Extremadura with little difficulty, the war wasn't to be as short as it might have appeared. Advancing on Madrid, he detoured to relieve the besieged garrison at Toledo; by the time he turned his attention back to the capital, the defences had been shored up and Madrid resisted throughout the war.

A key aspect of the Spanish Civil War was international involvement. Fascist Germany and Italy had troops to test and and a range of weaponry to play with, and these countries gave massive aid to the Nationalist cause as a rehearsal for World War II, which was appearing increasingly inevitable. Russia provided the Republicans with some material, but inscrutable Stalin never committed his full support. Other countries, such as Britain, the USA and France, disgracefully maintained a charade of international non-intervention despite the flagrant breaches by the above nations. Notwithstanding, thousands of volunteers mobilised to form the international brigades to assist the Republicans. Enlisting for idealistic reasons to combat the rise of fascism, many of these soldiers were writers and poets such as George Orwell and WH Auden.

Although Republican territory was split geographically, far more damage was done to their cause by ongoing and bitter infighting between anarchists, socialists, Soviet-backed communists and independent communists. There was constant struggling for power, political manoeuvring, backstabbing and outright violence, which the well-organised Nationalists must have watched with glee. The climax came in Barcelona in May 1937, when the Communist party took up arms against the anarchists and the POUM, an independent communist group. The city declined into a mini civil war of its own until order was restored. Morale, however, had taken a fatal blow.

Cities continued to fall to the Nationalists, for whom the German Condor legion proved a decisive force. In the south, the armies were under the command of Gonzalo Quelpo de Llano, who though of broadly republican sympathies, was one of the original conspirators, and had expertly and brutally taken Seville at the beginning of the Civil War. His propaganda broadcasts throughout the war revealed him to be a psychopathic sadist who encouraged his troops to rape, torture and murder, and who consistently lied about the war's progress; he took Málaga in early 1937. Fleeing refugees were massacred by tanks and aircraft. Republican hopes now rested solely in the outbreak of a Europe-wide war. Franco had set up base appropriately in deeply conservative Burgos; Nationalist territory was the venue for many brutal reprisals against civilians perceived as leftist, unionist, democratic, or owning a tasty little piece of land on the edge of the village. Republican atrocities in many areas were equally appalling although rarely sanctioned or perpetrated by the government.

The Republicans made a couple of last-ditch efforts in early 1938 at Teruel and in the Ebro valley, but were beaten in some of the most gruelling fighting of the Civil War. The Nationalists reached the Mediterranean, dividing Catalunya from the rest of Republican territory and, after the ill-fated Republican offensive over the Ebro put Barcelona under intense pressure, it finally fell in January 1939. Even at this late stage, given united resistance, the Republicans could have held out a while longer and World War II might have prevented a Franco victory, but it wasn't to be. The fighting spirit had largely dissipated and the infighting led to meek capitulation. Franco entered Madrid and the war was declared over on 1 April 1939.

If Republicans were hoping that this would signal the end of the slaughter and bloodshed, they didn't know the *generalísimo* well enough. A vengeful spate of executions, lynchings, imprisonments and torture ensued, and the dull weight of the new regime stifled growth and optimism. Although many thousands of Spaniards fought in World War II (on both sides), Spain remained nominally neutral. After meeting Franco at Hendaye, Hitler declared that he would prefer to have three or four teeth removed than have to do so again. Franco had his eye on French Morocco and was hoping to be granted it for minimal Spanish involvement, but Hitler accurately realised that the country had little more to give in the way of war effort and didn't offer an alliance.

The post-war years were tough in Spain, particularly in poverty-stricken Andalucía, where the old system was back in place and the workers penniless and starving. Franco was an international outcast and many thousands of Andalucíans left in search of employment and a better life in Europe, the USA and Latin America. The Cold War was to prove Spain's saviour. Franco was nothing if not anti-communist and the USA began to see his potential as an ally. Eisenhower offered to provide a massive aid package in exchange for Spanish support against the Eastern Bloc. In practice, this meant the creation of American military bases on Spanish soil; one of the biggest is at Rota, just outside Cádiz.

The dollars were dirty, but the country made the most of them. Spain boomed in the 1960s as industry finally took off and the flood of tourism to the Andalucian coasts began in earnest. But dictatorship was no longer fashionable in western Europe and Spain was regarded as a slightly embarrassing cousin. It was not invited to join the European Economic Community (EEC) and it seemed as if nothing was going to really change until Franco died. He finally did, in 1975, and his appointed successor, King Juan Carlos I, the grandson of Alfonso XIII, took the throne of a country burning with democratic desires.

La Transición

The king was initially predicted to be just Franco's pet and therefore committed to maintaining the stultifying status quo, but he surprised everyone by acting swiftly to appoint the young Adolfo Suárez as prime minister. Suárez bullied the parliament into approving a new parliamentary system; political parties were legalised in 1977 and elections held in June that year. The return to democracy was known as *la transición*, and the accompanying cultural explosion became known as *la movida (madrileña)*. Suárez's centrist party triumphed and he continued his reforms. The 1978 constitution declared Spain a parliamentary monarchy with no official religion; Franco must have turned in his grave and Suárez faced increasing opposition from the conservative elements in his own party. He resigned in 1981 and, as his successor was preparing to take power, the good old Spanish tradition of the *pronunciamiento* came to the fore once again. A detachment of Guardia Civil stormed parliament under the leadership of Lieutenant Colonel Tejero. After a tense few hours, the king remained calm and, dressed in his capacity as head of the armed forces, assured the people of his commitment to democracy. The coup attempt thus failed and Juan Carlos was seen in an even better light.

In 1982, the Socialist government (PSOE) of Felipe González was elected. Hailing from Seville, he was committed to improving conditions and infrastructure in his native Andalucía. The single most important legislation since the return to democracy was the creation of the *comunidades autónomas*, in which the regions of Spain were given their own parliaments, which operate with varying degrees of freedom from the central government. This came to bear in 1983, although it was a process initiated by Suárez. Seville became the capital of the Andalucian region.

The Socialists held power for 14 years and oversaw Spain's entry into the EEC (now EU) in 1986, from which it has benefited immeasurably, although rural Andalucía remains poor by western European standards. But mutterings of several scandals began to plague the PSOE government and González was really disgraced when he was implicated in having commissioned death squads with the aim of terrorising the Basques into renouncing terrorism, which few of them supported in any case.

Modern Spain and Andalucía

In 1996, the rightist PP (Partido Popular), under **José María Aznar**, took over the reins from the Socialist government, and were re-elected in 2000. Economically conservative, Aznar strengthened Spain's ties with Europe. After the Madrid train bombings in 2004, wrongly attributed to ETA by Aznar, PSOE leader **José Luis Zapatero** was unexpectedly elected. His government outraged the right by legalising same-sex marriage and expedited divorce, granting the Catalan government more autonomy, and supporting victims of Franco and the Civil War with the Law of Historical Memory.

Zapatero's handling of 'la crisis' was widely criticised: the 2008 global economic downturn hit Andalucía especially hard, as construction collapsed, tourism suffered and unemployment soared to 25% (57% among young people).

The 15-M anti-austerity movement in 2011 resulted in PP leader **Mariano Rajoy** taking power as a stabilising force, although his deep social welfare cuts proved massively unpopular and a new radical left party founded by 15-M participants, **Podemos**, sprung up in response. Catalan independence remained a divisive issue.

Socialist **Pedro Sánchez** became PM in 2018 via a no-confidence vote after a PP corruption scandal (one of an endless succession on both sides). He has ruled in a coalition with Unidas Podemos and later Sumar, while a new extreme-right party, **Vox**, has capitalised on anti-immigrant sentiment. Sánchez has raised the minimum wage, passed feminist legislation and strengthened LGBTQIA+ protections.

Spain is currently Europe's fastest-growing economy, largely thanks to the migrants in its workforce. Andalucía itself has been transformed since the Transition, from a poor region reliant on agriculture into a largely urban society. EU development funds were used to modernise transport infrastructure (notably the AVE high-speed train to Seville, opened in time for Expo 1992). Seville has developed a significant aeronautical industry, while Andalucía enjoys a strong renewable energy sector (57% of the region's electricity is from renewable sources). Almería's 'plastic seas' of greenhouses dominate EU vegetable supply, though labour conditions remain controversial, especially for immigrants.

Today, chronic droughts and housing pressures in tourism zones are the major environmental and social challenges for Andalucía.

Culture

Architecture

Spain's architectural heritage is one of Europe's richest and certainly its most diverse, due in large part to the dual influences of European Christian and Islamic styles during the eight centuries of Moorish presence in the peninsula. Another factor is economic: both during the Reconquista and in the wake of the discovery of the Americas, money seemed limitless and vast building projects were undertaken. Entire treasure fleets were spent on erecting lavish churches and monasteries on previously Muslim soil, while the relationships with Islamic civilisation spawned some fascinating styles unique to Spain. The Moors adorned their towns with sensuous palaces and elegant mosques, as well as employing compact climate-driven urban planning that still forms the hearts of most towns. In modern times, Spain has shaken off the ponderous monumentalism of the Franco era and become something of a powerhouse of modern architecture.

The story of Spanish architecture really begins with the Romans, who colonised the peninsula and imposed their culture on it to a significant degree. More significant still is the legacy they left: architectural principles that endured and to some extent formed the basis for later peninsular styles.

There's not a wealth of outstanding monuments. **Itálica**, just outside Seville, is an impressive, if not especially well-preserved, Roman town. In many towns and villages you can see Roman fortifications and foundations under existing structures.

The first distinct period of Moorish architecture in Spain is that of the Umayyads who ruled as emirs, then as caliphs, from Córdoba from the eighth to 11th centuries. The period of the caliphate was the high point of Al-Andalus and some suitably sumptuous architecture remains.

The Almoravids contributed little to Andalucian architecture, but the Almohads brought their own architectural modifications with them. Based in Seville, their styles were not as flamboyant and relied heavily on ornamental brickwork. The supreme example of the period is the **Giralda tower** that once belonged to the mosque in Seville and now forms part of the cathedral. The use of intricate wood-panelled ceilings began to be popular and the characteristic Andalucian *azulejo* decorative tiles were first used at this time. Over this period, the horseshoe arch developed a point. The Almohads were great military architects and built or improved a large number of walls, fortresses and towers, which often have characteristic pointed battlements. The **Torre del Oro** in Seville is one of the most famous and attractive examples.

The climax of Moorish architecture ironically came when Al-Andalus was already doomed and had been reduced to the emirate of Granada. The Alcázar in Seville is a good example of the period, though actually constructed in Christian Spain; it is very Nasrid in character and Granadan craftsmen certainly worked on it.

As the Christians gradually took back Andalucía, they introduced their own styles, developed in the north with substantial influence from France and Italy. The Romanesque barely features in Andalucía; it was the Gothic style that influenced post-Reconquista church building in the 13th, 14th and 15th centuries. It was combined with styles learned under the Moors to form an Andalucian fusion known as Gothic-*mudéjar*. Many of the region's churches are constructed on these lines, typically featuring a rectangular floor plan with a triple nave surrounded by pillars, a polygonal chancel and square chapels. Gothic exterior buttresses were used and many had a bell-tower decorated with ornate brickwork reminiscent of the Giralda, which was also rebuilt during this period.

The Andalucian Gothic style differs from the rest of the peninsula in its basic principles. Whereas in the north, the 'more space, less stone, more light' philosophy pervaded, practical considerations demanded different solutions in the south. One of these was space: the cathedrals normally occupied the site of former mosques, which had square ground plans and were hemmed in by other buildings. Another was defence – churches and cathedrals had to be ready to double as fortresses in case of attack, so sturdy walls were of more importance than stained glass. Many of Andalucía's churches, built in the Gothic style, were heavily modified in succeeding centuries and present a blend of different architectures.

Mudéjar architecture spread quickly across Spain. Moorish architects and those who worked with them began to meld their Islamic tradition with the northern influences. The result is distinctive and pleasing, typified by the decorative use of brick and coloured tiles, with tall elegant bell-towers a particular highlight. Another common feature is the highly elaborate wooden panelled ceilings, some of which are masterpieces. The word *artesonado* describes the most characteristic type of these. The style became popular nationwide and, in certain areas, *mudéjar* remained a constant feature for over 500 years of building.

The final phase of Spanish Gothic was the Isabelline, or Flamboyant. Produced during and immediately after the reign of the Catholic Monarchs (hence the name), it borrowed decorative motifs from Islamic architecture to create an exuberant form characterised by highly elaborate façades carved with tendrils, sweeping curves and geometrical patterns.

The 16th century was a high point in Spanish power and wealth, when it expanded across the Atlantic, tapping riches that must have seemed limitless. Spanish Renaissance architecture reflected this, leading from the late Gothic style into the elaborate peninsular style known as Plateresque. Although the style originally relied heavily on Italian models, it soon took on specifically Spanish features. The word refers particularly to the façades of civil and religious buildings, characterised by decoration of shields and other heraldic motifs, as well as geometric and naturalistic patterns such as shells. The term comes from the word for silversmith, *platero*, as the level of intricacy of the stonework approached that of jewellery. Arches went back to the rounded and columns and piers became a riot of foliage and 'grotesque' scenes.

A classical revival put an end to much of the elaboration, as Renaissance architects concentrated on purity. To classical Greek features such as fluted columns and pediments were added large Italianate cupolas and domes. Spanish architects were apprenticed to Italian masters and returned to Spain with their ideas. Elegant interior patios in *palacios* are an especially attractive feature of the style, to be found across the country. Andalucía is a particularly rich storehouse of this style, where the master Diego de Siloé designed numerous cathedrals and churches. Fine 16th-century *palacios* can be found in nearly every town and city of Andalucía; often built in honey-coloured sandstone, these noble buildings were the homes of the aristocrats who had reaped the riches of the Reconquista and the new trade routes to the Americas.

The pure lines of this Renaissance classicism were soon to be transformed into a new style, Spanish Baroque. Although it started fairly soberly, it soon became rather ornamental, often being used to add elements to existing buildings. The Baroque was a time of great genius in architecture as in the other arts in Spain, as masters playfully explored the reaches of their imaginations – a strong reaction against the sober preceding style. Churches became ever larger, in part to justify the huge façades, and nobles indulged in one-upmanship, building ever grander *palacios*. The façades themselves are typified by such features as pilasters (narrow piers descending to a point) and niches to hold statues. Andalucía has a vast array of Baroque churches, and Seville in particular bristles with them. Smaller towns, such as Écija, are also well endowed, as they enjoyed significant agriculture-based prosperity during the period.

The Baroque became more ornate as time went on, reaching the extremes of Churrigueresque, named for the Churriguera brothers who worked in the late 17th and early 18th centuries. The result can be over-elaborate but on occasion transcendentally beautiful. Vine tendrils and cherubs decorate façades and *retablos*, which seem intent on breaking every classical norm, twisting here, upside-down there and at their best seeming to capture motion.

Neoclassicism, encouraged by a new interest in the ancient civilisations of Greece and Rome, was an inevitable reaction to such *joie de vivre*. It again resorted to the cleaner lines of antiquity, which were used this time for public spaces as well as civic and religious buildings. Many plazas and town halls in Spain are in this style, which tended to flourish in the cities that were thriving in the late 18th and 19th centuries. The best examples use symmetry to achieve beauty and elegance, such as Seville's tobacco factory, which bridges Baroque and neoclassical styles.

Awakened interest in the days of Al-Andalus led to the neo-Moorish (or neo-*mudéjar*) style being used for public buildings and private residences. The most evident example of this is the fine ensemble of buildings constructed in Seville for the 1929 Ibero-American exhibition. Budgets were thrown out the window and the lavish pavilions are sumptuously decorated.

Elegance and whimsy never seemed to play much part in fascist architecture, and during the Franco era Andalucía was subjected to an appalling series of ponderous concrete monoliths, all in the name of progress. A few avant-garde buildings managed to escape the drudgery from the 1950s on, but it was the dictator's death in 1975, followed by EEC membership in 1986, that really provided the impetus for change.

Andalucía is not at the forefront of Spain's modern architectural movements, but the World Expo in Seville in 1992 brought some of the big names in. Among the various innovative pavilions, Santiago Calatrava's sublime bridge stands out. The impressive Teatro de la Maestranza and public library also date from this period, while the newer Olympic stadium is a more recent offering. Seville's fantastic Las Setas (the Mushrooms) building, daringly built over a square in the old town, is one of the latest spectacular constructions as well as César Pelli's 180 m Torre Sevilla, the tallest building in Andalucía. Elsewhere, the focus has been on softening the harsh Francoist lines of the city's 20th-century expansions. In most places this has been quietly successful.

Art

In the first millennium BC, Iberian cultures produced fine jewellery from gold and silver, as well as some remarkable sculpture and ceramics. These influences derived from contact with trading posts set up by the Phoenicians, who also left artistic evidence of their presence, mostly in the port cities they established. Similarly, the Romans brought their own artistic styles to the peninsula and there are many cultural remnants, including some fine sculpture and a number of elaborate mosaic floors. Later, the Visigoths were skilled artists and craftspeople and produced many fine pieces, most notably in metalwork.

The majority of the artistic heritage left by the Moors is tied up in their architecture (see above). As Islamic tradition forbade the portrayal of human or animal figures, the norm was intricate applied decoration with calligraphic, geometric and vegetal themes predominating. Superb panelled ceilings are a feature of Almohad architecture, a particularly attractive style being that known as *artesonado*, in which the concave panels are bordered with elaborate inlay work. During this period, glazed tiles known as *azulejos* began to be produced, and these continue to be a feature of Andalucian craftsmanship.

The gradual process of the Reconquista brought Christian styles into Andalucía. Generally speaking, the Gothic, which had arrived in Spain both overland from France and across the Mediterranean from Italy, was the first post-Moorish style in Andalucía. Over time, Gothic sculpture achieved greater naturalism and became more ornate, culminating in the technical mastery of sculptors and painters such as Pedro Millán, Pieter Dancart (who is responsible for the massive *retablo*, or altarpiece, of Seville's cathedral) and Alejo Fernández, all of whom were from or heavily influenced by northern Europe.

Although, to begin with, the finest artists were working in northern Spain, Andalucía soon could boast several notable figures of its own. In the wake of the Christian conquest of Granada, the Catholic Monarchs and their successor Carlos V went on a building spree. The Spanish Renaissance drew heavily on the Italian but developed its own style. Perhaps the finest 16th-century figure is Pedro de Campaña, a Fleming whose exalted talent went largely unrecognised in his own time. His altarpiece of the Purification of Mary in Seville's cathedral is particularly outstanding.

As the Renaissance progressed, naturalism in painting increased, leading into the Golden Age of Spanish art. As Seville prospered on New World riches, the city became a centre for artists, who found wealthy patrons in abundance. Pre-eminent among all was Diego Rodríguez de Silva Velázquez (1599-1660), who started his career there before moving to Madrid to become a court painter. Another remarkable painter working in Seville was Francisco de Zurbarán (1598-1664), whose idiosyncratic style often focuses on superbly rendered white garments in a dark, brooding background, a metaphor for the subjects themselves, who were frequently priests. During Zurbarán's later years, he was eclipsed in the Seville popularity stakes by Bartolomé Esteban Murillo (1618-1682). While at first glance his paintings can seem heavy on the sentimentality, they tend to focus on the space between the central characters, who interact with glances or gestures of great power and meaning. Juan Valdés Leal painted many churches and monasteries in Seville; his greatest works are the macabre realist paintings in the Hospital de la Caridad. The sombre tone struck by these works reflects the decline of the once-great mercantile city.

At this time, the sculptor Juan Martínez Montañés carved numerous figures, *retablos* and *pasos* (ornamental floats for religious processions) in wood. Pedro Roldán, Juan de Mesa and Pedro de Mena were other important Baroque sculptors from this period, as was Alonso Cano, a crotchety but talented painter and sculptor working from Granada. The main focus of this medium continued to be ecclesiastic: *retablos* became ever larger and more ornate, commissioned by nobles to gain favour with the church and improve their chances in the afterlife.

The 18th and early 19th centuries saw fairly characterless art produced under the new dynasty of Bourbon kings. Tapestry production increased markedly but never scaled the heights of the earlier Flemish masterpieces. One man who produced pictures for tapestries was the master of 19th-century art, Francisco Goya, a remarkable figure whose finest works included both paintings and etchings. There's a handful of his work scattered around Andalucía's galleries, but the best examples are in Madrid's Prado and in the north.

After Goya, the 19th century produced few works of note as Spain tore itself apart in a series of brutal conflicts. In response to this, the *costumbrista* tradition developed with painters and writers focusing on portraying Spanish life, their depictions often revolving around nostalgia and stereotypes. Among the best were the Bécquer family: José, his cousin Joaquín, and his son Valeriano, whose brother Gustavo Adolfo was one of the period's best-known poets.

The Civil War was to have a serious effect on art in Spain, as a majority of artists sided with the Republic and fled Spain with their defeat. Picasso's *Guernica* is a powerful anti-war painting; Dalí and Miró also produced war-themed works. Franco was far from an enlightened patron of the arts and his occupancy was a monotonous time. Today's local governments are more supportive of art, and the museums in each provincial capital usually have a good collection of modern works. Seville's Centro Andaluz de Arte Contemporáneo (page 36) is well worth a visit.

Literature

One of the most remarkable of Spain's literary figures was the 7th-century bishop of Seville, San Isidoro, whose works were classic texts for over a millennium.

The extraordinary life of Miguel de Cervantes (1547-1616) marks the start of a rich period of Spanish literature. *Don Quijote* came out in serial form in 1606 and is rightly considered one of the finest novels ever written; it's certainly the widest-read Spanish work. Cervantes spent plenty of time in Andalucía and some of his *Novelas Ejemplares* are short stories set in Seville.

The Sevillian Lope de Rueda (1505-1565) was in many ways Spain's first playwright. He wrote comedies and paved the way for the explosion of Spanish drama under the big three – Lope de Vega, Tirso de Molina and Calderón de la Barca – when public theatres opened in the early 17th century.

The 18th century was not such a rich period for Andalucian or Spanish writing, but in the 19th century the *costumbrista* movement (see page 82) produced several fine works, among them *La Gaviota* (the Seagull) by Fernán Caballero, who was actually a Seville-raised woman named Cecilia Böhl von Faber, and *Escenas Andaluzas* (Andalucian Scenes), by Serafín Estébanez Calderón. Gustavo Adolfo Bécquer, who was born in Seville, died young having published a famous series of legends and just one volume of poetry containing popular, yearning works about love.

At the end of the 19th century, Spain lost the last of its colonial possessions after revolts and a war with the USA. This event, known as the Disaster, had a profound impact on the nation and its date 1898 gave its name to a generation of writers and artists. This group sought to express what Spain was and had been, and to achieve new perspectives for the 20th century.

The Generation of '27, another loose grouping of artists and writers, included neo-romantic Sevillano poets Luis Cernuda (1902-1963) and Vicente Aleixandre (1898-1984), winner of the 1977 Nobel Prize for his surrealist-influenced free verse. The most celebrated of this group was, of course, Granadan poet and playwright Federico García Lorca.

Music and dance

Flamenco

Few things symbolise the mysteries of Andalucía like flamenco but, as with the region itself, much has been written that is over-romanticised, patronising or just plain untrue. Like bullfighting, flamenco as we know it is a fairly young art, having basically developed in the 19th century, with roots in gypsy, Jewish and Arabic music. It is constantly evolving and there have been significant changes in its performance in the last century, which makes the search for classic flamenco a bit of a wild goose chase. Rather, the element to search for is authentic emotion and, beyond this, *duende*, an undefinable passion that carries singer and watchers away in a whirlwind of raw feeling, with a devil-may-care sneer at destiny.

Though there have been many excellent *payo* flamenco artists, its history is primarily a gypsy one. It was developed among the gypsy population in the

Seville and Cádiz area but clearly includes elements of cultures encountered when the gypsies migrated from India to Europe 600 years ago.

Flamenco consists of three basic components: *el cante* (the song), *el toque* (the guitar) and *el baile* (the dance). In addition, *el jaleo* provides percussion sounds through shouts, clicking fingers, *palmas* (clapping) and footwork (and, less traditionally, castanets); a *cajón* (a wooden box on which the musician sits, using taps, slaps and knocks to create rhythmic sounds) is increasingly used in *tablaos*. Flamenco can be divided into four basic types: *tonás*, *siguiriyas*, *soleá* and *tangos*, which are characterised by their *compás* or form, rhythm and accentuation, and are either *cante jondo* (emotionally deep)/*cante grande* (big) or *cante chico* (small). Related to flamenco, but not in a pure form, are *sevillanas*, danced till you drop at the Feria.

For a foreigner, perhaps the classic image of flamenco is a woman in a theatrical dress clicking castanets. A more authentic image is of a singer and guitarist, both sitting rather disconsolately on painted chairs, or perhaps on a wooden box (*cajón*, see above) to tap out a rhythm. The singer and the guitarist work together, sensing the mood of the other and improvising. A beat is provided by clapping of hands or tapping of feet. If there's a dancer, he or she will dictate the pace and mood. The dancing is stop-start, frenetic: the flamenco can reach crescendos of frightening emotional intensity when it seems the singer will have a stroke, the dancer is about to commit murder, and the guitarist may never find it back to the world of the sane. These outbursts of passion are seen to their fullest in *cante jondo*, the deepest and saddest form of flamenco.

After going through a moribund period during the mid-20th century, flamenco was revived by such revered Andalucian artists as Paco de Lucía, and the gaunt, heroin-addicted genius Camarón de la Isla – their revolutionary 'new flamenco' combined the genre with blues, pop and rock – while the flamenco theatre of Joaquín Cortés put purists' noses firmly out of joint but achieved worldwide popularity. More recently, Diego 'El Cigala' carries on Camarón's angst-ridden tradition. Flamenco-blues fusion was also made popular by Seville brothers Raimundo and Rafael Amador. Contemporary dancers such as Israel Galván and Rocío Molina are breaking the mould with avant-garde approaches, while Rosalía is the latest singer to find international success reinterpreting flamenco by fusing it with pop and other genres. Flamenco was given a massive boost in visibility when it was recognised as UNESCO Intangible World Heritage. Seville's Bienal de Flamenco (Sep–Oct, even-numbered years) is the perfect place to see the latest shows. Obviously the most famous musical depiction of Seville is in Bizet's iconic opera *Carmen*, set in the Tobacco Factory and bullring, among other locations.

Religion and beliefs

The history of Spain and the history of the Spanish Catholic church are barely separable but, in 1978, Article 16 of the new constitution declared that Spain was now a nation without an official religion, less than a decade after Franco's right hand man, Admiral Luis Carrero Blanco, had declared that 'Spain is Catholic or she is nothing'.

From the sixth-century writings of San Isidoro onwards, the destiny of Spain was a specifically Catholic one. The Reconquista was a territorial war inspired by holy zeal, Jews and Moors were expelled in the quest for pure Catholic blood, the Inquisition demonstrated the young nation's religious insecurities and paranoias and Felipe II bled Spain dry pursuing futile wars in a vain attempt to protect his beloved Church from the spread of Protestantism. Much of the strife of the 1800s was caused by groups attempting to end or defend the power of the church, while in the 20th century the fall of the Second Republic and the Civil War was engendered partly by the provocatively anticlerical actions of the leftists.

Faced with a census form, 53% of Spaniards claim to be Catholics, but less than a third of that number cut regular figures in the parish church. Although consistent churchgoing is increasingly confined to an aged (mostly female) segment of society and seminaries struggle to produce enough priests to stock churches, it's not the whole picture. *Romerías* (religious processions to rural chapels and sites) and religious fiestas are well attended, and places of pilgrimage, usually chapels housing venerated statues of the Virgin, are flooded with Spanish visitors during the summer months. At Easter, a big percentage of the population of some towns participates in solemn processions of religious *cofradías* (brotherhoods), most famously in Seville. Nevertheless, the church plays an increasingly minor role in most Spaniards' lives, especially of those born after the return to democracy, and these days, most weddings (around 75-80%) are conducted away from the church's bosom.

In terms of other religions, according to the latest figures, there are around 2.4 to 3 million Muslims in Spain, around 5% of the population.

Practicalities

Getting there

There are numerous options for reaching Seville. As well as Seville airport, you can fly into Málaga or Gibraltar.

Both legacy and budget airlines have routes to Seville; the latter's fares are lower and they operate from more regional airports, but they can depart at antisocial hours.

Before booking, it's worth doing a bit of online research. Three of the best search engines for flight comparisons are www.opodo.com, www.skyscanner.com and www.kayak.com, which compare prices from different airlines. To keep up to date with the ever-changing routes available, sites like www.flightmapper.net are handy. **Flightchecker** ⓘ *http://flightchecker.moneysavingexpert.com* is handy for checking multiple dates for budget airline deals.

Flights from the UK

Competition has benefited travellers in recent years. Budget operators have taken a significant slice of the market and forced other airlines to compete.

Budget There are numerous budget connections from the UK to Seville and Málaga. **Easyjet** and **Ryanair** fly from over a dozen UK airports, while other budget airlines running various routes from the UK include **Flybe**, **Vueling**, **Norwegian**, **Jet2** and **Wizz Air**.

Charter There are numerous charter flights to Málaga from many British and Irish airports. **TUI** ⓘ *www.tui.co.uk* is probably the best charter-flight provider.

Non-budget flights Málaga again has the most scheduled flights, with several legacy airlines including **Iberia** and **British Airways** flying direct from London airports and a few other UK cities. From London, there are daily direct flights to Seville.

Flights from the rest of Europe

There are numerous budget airlines operating from European and Spanish cities to Málaga and Seville.

Numerous charter flights operate to Málaga from Germany, Scandinavia, France, the Netherlands and Belgium.

There are direct flights to Málaga with non-budget airlines from many major European cities, as well as to Seville from a growing number of European capitals. Flying from these or other western European cities via Madrid or Barcelona usually costs about the same.

Packing for Seville

Spain is a modern European country, and you can buy almost everything you'll need here; packing light is the way to go. A GPS device is handy for navigating and a European adaptor (plug a double adaptor into it) is a must for recharging electrical goods (see page 101). Some accommodation has USB sockets.

Flights from North America and Canada

United flies direct from New York to Málaga, while there are thrice-weekly flights from Montreal and Toronto with **Air Transat**. Otherwise, you'll have to connect via Madrid, Barcelona, Lisbon, London or another European city to Andalucian airports. Although sometimes you'll pay little extra to Andalucía than the Madrid flight, you can often save considerably by flying to Madrid and getting the bus down south, or book a domestic connection on the local no-frills airline **Vueling** ⓘ *www.vueling.com*, or **Ryanair** ⓘ *www.ryanair.com*.

Flights from Australia and New Zealand

There are no direct flights to Spain from Australia or New Zealand; the cheapest and quickest way is to connect via Frankfurt, Paris or London. It might turn out cheaper to book the Europe–Spain leg separately via a budget operator.

Road

Bus

FlixBus ⓘ *www.flixbus.co.uk* runs several buses from major European cities to Seville, but you won't get there cheaper than a flight. A good price comparison website is *www.omio.com*.

Car and sea

It's a long haul to Seville by road if you're not already in the peninsula. From the UK, you have two options if you want to take the car: a ferry to northern Spain (www.brittany-ferries.co.uk), or cross the Channel to France and then drive down. The former option is much more expensive; it would usually work out far cheaper to fly to Seville and hire a car once you get there. For competitive fares by sea to France and Spain, check with **Ferrysavers** ⓘ *www.ferrysavers.com* or **Direct Ferries** ⓘ *www.directferries.com*.

Seville is about 2000 km from London by road; a dedicated drive will get you there in 20-24 driving hours. By far the fastest route is to head down the west coast of France and to Burgos via San Sebastián. From here, head for Salamanca then south.

Train

Unless you've got a rail pass, love train travel or aren't too keen on planes, forget about getting to Seville by train from anywhere further than France; you'll save no money over the plane fare and use up days of time better spent in tapas bars. You'll have to connect via either Barcelona or Madrid. Getting to Madrid/Barcelona from London takes about a day using **Eurostar** ⓘ *www.eurostar.com, £78-380 return to Paris*, and another €250 or more return to reach Madrid/Barcelona from there. Using the train/Channel ferry combination might be cheaper but will double the time to Paris.

If you are planning the train journey, **Voyages-SNCF** ⓘ *www.sncf-connect.com*, is a useful company. **Renfe**, Spain's rail network, has online timetables at www.renfe.com. Best of all is the extremely useful **www.seat61.com**.

Getting around

Bus

Buses are the staple of Spanish public transport. Services between major cities are fast, frequent, reliable and fairly cheap: the six-hour trip from Madrid to Seville, for example, costs from about €27 one way. When buying a ticket, always check how long the journey will take, as the odd bus will be an 'all stations to' job, calling in at villages that seem surprised to even see it.

Most towns and cities have a single terminal, the *estación de autobuses* (Seville has two: Plaza de Armas and Prado de San Sebastián). Buy your ticket at the relevant window; if there isn't one, buy it from the driver; alternatively book it online. Superior classes may cost up to 60% more but offer lounge access and onboard service. Newer buses in all classes may offer Wi-Fi, personal entertainment system and sockets. Most tickets will have an *asiento* (seat number) on them; ask when buying the ticket if you prefer a *ventana* (window) or *pasillo* (aisle) seat. If you're travelling at busy times (particularly a fiesta or national holiday), always book the bus ticket in advance.

Rural bus services are slower, less frequent and more difficult to co-ordinate.

All bus services are reduced on Sundays and, to a lesser extent, on Saturdays; some services don't run at all on weekends.

Car

Roads and motorways While driving in Spain isn't as sedate as in parts of northern Europe, it's generally pretty good and you'll have few problems.

There are two types of motorway in Spain, *autovías* and *autopistas*; for drivers, they are little different. They are signposted in blue and may have tolls (*peajes*) payable, in which case there'll be a red warning circle when you're entering the AP (*autopista de pago*, toll motorway). Tolls are generally reasonable; the quality of motorway is generally excellent. The speed limit on motorways is 120 km/h.

Rutas Nacionales form the backbone of the country's road network. Centrally administered, they vary in quality. Typically, they are choked with traffic backed up behind trucks, and there are few stretches of dual carriageway. Driving at siesta time is a good idea if you're going to be on a busy stretch. Rutas Nacionales are marked with a red N followed by a number. The speed limit is 90 km/h outside built-up areas, as it is for secondary roads, which are usually marked with an A (Andalucía), or provincial (eg SE for Sevilla) prefix.

In urban areas, the speed limit is 30 km/h (50 km/h with two lanes), except where signs indicate a lower limit. City driving can be confusing, with signposting generally poor and traffic heavy; it's worth using a navigation app such as Google Maps on the car's screen via your phone. In some towns and cities, many of the hotels are officially signposted, making things easier. Larger cities may have their historic quarter blocked off by barriers or monitored by cameras. Check with your hotel before arriving about how to access it by car. A small number have on-site parking, while others have an arrangement with a nearby underground car park. A few offer valet parking – a most welcome touch with such heart-stoppingly narrow streets.

Be aware that the interior part of La Cartuja in Seville is a ZBE or low-emission zone (the city centre may follow, so check for updates on sevilla.org/servicios/movilidad). Police are increasingly enforcing speed limits in Spain, and foreign drivers are liable to a large on-the-spot fine. As of 2026, all drivers in Spain must carry a V16 emergency beacon, a small orange flashing light with a geolocator that is magnetically attached to the car's roof in case of a breakdown. You also need a set of spare bulbs with relevant tools, and a yellow high-vis vest. Drink driving is being cracked down on; the limit is 0.5 g/l of blood, a little lower than the equivalent in the UK, for example. Electric cars are widely used, and EV drivers will find over 300 charging points in Seville, in hotels and underground car parks, including in shopping centres.

Parking Parking is a problem in nearly every town and city in Seville province. Red or yellow lines on the side of the street mean no parking. Blue or white lines mean that some restrictions are in place; a sign will indicate what these are (typically it means that the parking is metered). Parking meters can usually only be dosed up for a maximum of one to three hours, but they take a siesta at lunchtime too, as well as Saturday afternoons and all day Sunday. Print the ticket off and display it in the car. If you overstay and get fined, you can pay it off for minimal cost at the machine if you do it within an hour of the fine being issued. If it's a hire car you'll likely be liable for the fine. Underground car parks are common, but pricey; €17-30 a day is normal. The website www.parkopedia.es is useful for locating underground car parks and comparing their rates.

Documentation To drive in Spain, you'll need a full driving licence from your home country. This applies to virtually all foreign nationals but, in practice, if you're from an 'unusual' country, consider an International Driving Licence or official translation of your licence into Spanish.

Liability insurance is required for every car driven in Spain and you must carry proof of it. If bringing your own car, check carefully with your insurers that you're covered and get a certificate (green card).

Car hire Hiring a car is easy and cheap. The major multinationals have offices at all large towns and airports. Prices start at around €50 per week for a small car with unlimited mileage. You'll need a credit card and most agencies will either not accept under-25s or demand a surcharge. By far the cheapest place to hire a car is the airport – Seville or Málaga. With the bigger companies, it's always cheaper to book over the internet. The best way to look for a deal is using a price-comparison website, such as www.clickrent.es.

You can often choose between full to full petrol tank (more economical) or full to empty (more convenient). Bring both USB-A and USB-C cables as your rental car might have either socket.

Cycling and motorcycling

Motorcycling is a good way to enjoy Seville and there are few difficulties to trouble the biker; bike shops and mechanics are relatively common. There are comparatively few outlets for motorcycle hire. Electric moped hire is popular: try Acciona ⓘ *www.movilidad.acciona.com* or Yego ⓘ *www.rideyego.com.*

Spaniards are mad for competitive cycling and it has grown in popularity as a means of transport; local governments are encouraging this with bike lanes and rental bikes in cities, thus there are plenty of cycling shops. Taking your own bike to Seville is well worth the effort as most airlines are happy to accept them, providing they come within your baggage allowance. Bikes can be taken on the train, but may have to be dismantled, and must be booked on most services. Alternatively, you can rent a (traditional or electric) bike (www.rentabikesevilla. com) or moped (www.rideyego.com or www.movilidad.acciona.com) and zip around the streets like a local. For motorbike hire, try www.momomoven.es.

Hitchhiking and ride-sharing

Hitchhiking is uncommon in Spain, largely because it is not allowed on motorways; on a *nacional* (main road) or local road, however, you might get lucky. Ride-sharing is a popular way to get around cheaply; Blablacar ⓘ *www.blablacar.e*s is a good bet.

Taxi and bus

Seville city and the provincial towns have their sights closely packed into the centre, so you won't find local buses particularly necessary. There's a fairly comprehensive network in most towns, though, and the travel text indicates where they come in handy. Taxis are a good option: the minimum charge is around €4-5 in most places (it increases slightly at night and on Sundays). A taxi is available if its green light is lit; hail one on the street, call, or ask for the nearest *parada de taxis* (rank). If you're using a cab to get to somewhere beyond the city limits, there are fixed tariffs. Uber and Cabify both operate in Seville and Málaga: order rides via their apps. Preset prices can be steeper when demand is high.

Train

The Spanish national rail network, **Renfe** ⓘ *T912-320320 (English-speaking operators), www.renfe.com for timetables and tickets*, is, thanks to its growing network of high-speed trains, a useful option. **AVE** trains run from Madrid to Seville and, though expensive, cover this large distance impressively quickly and reliably. New, more economical high-speed services Avlo (low-price AVE), Ouigo ⓘ *www.ouigo.co*m and Iryo ⓘ *www.iryo.es* offer competitive rates. Compare schedules and prices on www.omio.com.

With Renfe, prices vary significantly according to the type of service you are using. Services are labelled Alvia and Intercity for long distance, and Avant and Media Distancia for medium distance. Slower local trains are called Regionales, and Cercanías are suburban trains.

It's always worth buying tickets in advance for long-distance travel, because trains are often full. The best option is to buy them via the respective website or app, which sometimes offers advance purchase discounts. You can download the ticket, with QR code, to your phone; print out the ticket yourself; or print it at a railway station using the reservation code. If buying your ticket at the station, allow plenty of time for queuing. Ticket windows are labelled *venta anticipada* (at least one day before travel) and *venta inmediata* (for travel on the same day).

All Spanish trains are non-smoking. The faster trains will have first-class (*preferente*) and second-class sections as well as a cafeteria. First class costs about 30% more than standard and can be a worthwhile deal on a crowded long journey. Families and groups can take advantage of the cheap '*mesa*' tickets, where you reserve four seats around a table. Buying a return ticket (*ida y vuelta*) is up to 30% cheaper than two singles, but you qualify for this discount even if you buy the return leg later (but not on every service).

An **ISIC student card** or **youth card** grants a discount of 5%-20% on train services. If you're using a European rail pass, be aware that you'll still have to make a reservation on Spanish trains and pay the small reservation fee (which covers your insurance). If you have turned 60, it's worth paying €6 for a Tarjeta Dorada, a seniors' card that gets you a discount of 25% on trains from Monday to Friday, and 40% at other times.

Maps

A useful website for route planning is www.guiarepsol.com. Car hire companies have satnavs available, though they charge a hefty supplement. Most cars have display screens that link to mobile phones, so it's easier to just plug in your phone (bring both types of USB cable) and use a navigation app like Google Maps ⓘ *www.maps.google.com.*

Where to stay

from hotels and hostels to apartments

The standard of accommodation in Seville is very high, with even the most modest of *pensiones* usually very clean and respectable. At time of writing, for Spain the website www.booking.com is by far the most comprehensive and has the best rates; www.hotels.com and www.laterooms.com have some good deals too, as does www.airbnb.com. Sometimes, booking direct with the hotel can get you special rates and extras, plus some travellers prefer to avoid less scrupulous mega-booking sites. The thorny issue of self-catering accommodation affects Seville as it does other tourist-swamped cities, and short-term rentals have been limited in the most popular areas to protect residents' long-term rental options.

Opting for more sustainable tourism choices – picking a *casa rural* in a traditional village or a hotel with a conscientious environmental and sustainability policy, including energy efficiency, water conservation, using renewable energy and a commitment to reduce waste – can reduce your footprint.

Types of accommodation

Hostales, pensiones and hostels

Hostales go from one to two stars. The *hostal* category includes *pensiones*, the standard budget option, typically family-run; hostels, aimed at younger travellers, have both shared dorms and private rooms. The standard for the price paid is normally excellent, and they're nearly all spotless. Spanish traditions of hospitality are alive and well; check-out time is almost uniformly a very civilised midday.

Hotels

A great number of Spanish hotels are well equipped but somewhat characterless chain business places (big players include **NH** ⓘ *www.nh-hoteles.es,* **AC/Marriott** ⓘ *www.ac-hotels.marriott.com,* **Melia** ⓘ *www.melia.com,* **Eurostars** ⓘ *www.eurostarshotels.com* and **Radisson** ⓘ *www.radissonhotels.com*), and can be

Price codes

Where to stay	Restaurants
€€€€ over €200	€€€ over €40
€€€ €120-200	€€ €20-40
€€ €75-120	€ under €20
€ under €75	
A standard double/twin room in high season.	A two-course meal for one person, without drinks.

found in and around the centre of Seville city. This guide has expressly minimised these in the listings, preferring to concentrate on more atmospheric options.

Casas rurales

An excellent option if you've got your own transport are the networks of rural houses, called *casas rurales*. The best of them are traditional farmhouses or characterful village cottages. Some are available only to rent out whole (often for a minimum of three days), while others offer rooms on a nightly basis. Rates tend to be excellent compared to hotels. Local tourist offices will have details; the tourist board lists a good selection on www.andalucia.org.

Youth hostels

There's a network of *albergues* (youth hostels), which are listed at www.inturjoven.com. These are institutional and often group-booked. Funding issues mean that many now open only seasonally. Major cities have backpacker hostels.

Campsites

Most campsites are set up as well-equipped holiday villages for families; some are open only in summer. While the facilities are good, they get extremely busy in peak season. Many have cabins or bungalows available, ranging from simple huts to houses with fully equipped kitchens and bathrooms. Don't camp where you're not allowed to: prohibitions are usually there for a good reason. Fire danger can be high in summer, so respect local regulations.

Self-catering

You'll find a huge variety of apartments to rent in Seville, from rooms and studios to stylish pads and luxurious palaces with private pools. As well as www.airbnb.com, try www.vrbo.com and veoapartment.com.

Prices

Price codes refer to a standard double or twin room, inclusive of IVA (VAT). The rates are generally for high season (March-May in Seville city). Occasionally, an area or town will have a short period when prices are hugely exaggerated; this is usually due to a festival such as Semana Santa (Holy Week) or a local *feria* (annual fair).

Breakfast is usually a generous spread, but pricey; you can choose a rate that includes it. Smaller independent hotels may include breakfast in the price if booking direct. Normally only the more expensive hotels have parking, and they always charge for it, normally around €20-25 per day.

All registered accommodation charges 10% VAT, which is usually included in the price. If you have any problems, a last resort is to ask for the *libro de reclamaciones* (complaints book) to fill in. Be aware that you must also take a copy to the local consumers' association for the complaint to be registered.

Food & drink

In few countries around the world are culture and society as intimately connected with eating and drinking as in Spain, and in Seville, the spiritual home of tapas, this is even more the case.

Food *See page 114 for a glossary of food.*

Cooking in Seville is characterised by an abundance of fresh ingredients, generally consecrated with the chef's holy trinity of garlic, onions and local olive oil.

The classic Andalucian breakfast is a *tostada* (a large toasted roll), traditionally slathered in olive oil, crushed tomato and *jamón ibérico*; avocado toast is now a veggie menu staple. For the sweet-toothed, *tostada* with jam or a pastry hits the mark, washed down with fresh orange juice. Brunch places are ubiquitous in cities and bigger towns. A common breakfast or afternoon snack are *churros*, fried dough sticks typically dipped in hot chocolate.

Lunch is the main meal and is nearly always a filling affair with three courses. Most places open for lunch at about 1300, and take last orders at 1500 or 1530, although at weekends this can extend. Lunchtime is the cheapest time to eat if you opt for the ubiquitous *menú del día*, usually a set three-course meal that includes wine or soft drink, typically costing €10 to €16. Dinner and/or evening tapas time is from around 2100 to midnight. It's not much fun sitting alone in a restaurant so try to adapt to the local hours: it may feel strange dining so late, but you'll miss out on a lot of atmosphere if you don't. If a place is open for lunch at noon, or dinner at 1900, it's likely to be a tourist trap.

Types of eatery

The great joy of eating out in Seville is going for tapas. This word refers to bar food, served in saucer-sized tapa portions typically costing €3-6. Tapas are available at lunchtime, but the classic time to eat them is in the evening. To do tapas the Andalucian way, don't order more than a couple at each place, taste each others' dishes, and stand at the bar. Locals know what the specialities of each bar are; if there's a daily special, order that. Also available are *raciones*, substantial meal-sized plates of the same fare, which also come in halves, *medias raciones*. Both are good for sharing. Considering these, the distinction between restaurants and tapas bars more or less disappears, because in the latter you can usually sit down at a table to order your *raciones*, effectively turning the experience into a meal. In terms of style, classic tapas bars will be adorned with hanging hams, bulls' heads and Semana Santa posters, while gastro bars – with modern takes on small dishes – will be more contemporary, ie minimalist, in décor.

Other types of eateries include a *freiduría*, a takeaway specialising in fried fish, while a *marisquería* is a classier type of seafood restaurant. In rural areas, look out for *ventas*, roadside eateries that often have a long history of feeding the passing muleteers with generous, hearty and cheap portions. The more cars and trucks outside, the better it will be. In Seville city, North African-style tea-houses, *teterías*, are popular.

Vegetarian food

Vegetarians in Seville won't be spoiled for choice, but at least what there is tends to be good. There are few dedicated vegetarian restaurants but most places will have a vegetarian main course on offer, and the existence of tapas, *raciones* and salads helps to extend the options available. Menus will generally feature one or more of: *tortilla* (potato omelette), spinach and chickpeas, vegetarian croquettes, tomato salad, or another potato dish. You'll have to specify *soy vegetariano/a* (I am a vegetarian), but ask what dishes contain because ham, fish and even chicken are often considered suitable vegetarian fare; you could also ask for some dishes without the meat/fish element. Vegans will have a tougher time: what doesn't have meat nearly always contains cheese or egg. Better restaurants, particularly in Seville city, will be happy to prepare something, but otherwise stick to very simple dishes.

On the menu

Typical starters include *gazpacho* (a cold summer tomato soup with garlic, cucumber and peppers, while *salmorejo* is a thicker version from Córdoba).

Raciones will usually be either meat or fish and are rarely served with side vegetables, apart from chips, although the dish itself may feature vegetables. Pork is widespread; *solomillo de cerdo*, *secreto*, *carrillada/carrillera*, *pluma* and *lomo* are all tasty cuts. Innards such as *callos* (tripe), *mollejas* (sweetbreads) and *morcilla* (black pudding) are excellent, if acquired tastes. Beef is less common. Note that Spaniards eat their steaks rare (*poco hecho*); for medium rare, ask for *al punto*, and *muy hecho* for well done. Chicken wings are popular, and *pollo* is also a common fixture in rice dishes. Salad bowls, with grains, seeds and raw vegetables, are increasingly common; vegetarians get tofu or seitan.

Seafood is the pride of Andalucía. The region is famous for its *pescaíto frito* (fried fish) which typically consists of battered anchovies (*boquerones*), squid (*calamares*), *choco* (cuttlefish) and dogfish (*cazón*). Shellfish include *mejillones* (mussels), *gambas* (prawns) and *almejas* (clams). *Chipirones* (small squid) are common, as well as *pulpo* (octopus). Among the vertebrates, *merluza* (hake) is the most widely used; *sardinas* (sardines), *dorada* (gilthead bream), *rape* (monkfish) and *pez espada* (swordfish) are all usually excellent. Look out for *atún de almadraba*, the finest quality, sustainably caught tuna from the Huelva and Cádiz coasts. It is best served raw as tartare, which features on many menus.

Signature tapas dishes vary from bar to bar and from province to province, and part of the delight of Seville comes in trying their specialities. Ubiquitous are *jamón* (cured ham; the best, *ibérico*, comes from purebred black-footed acorn-eating pigs that roam the woods of Huelva province and Extremadura) and *queso* (usually the hard salty *manchego* from Castilla-la Mancha; be sure to try rich, tangy Payoyo goat's cheese from Cádiz.). *Gambas* (prawns) are usually on the tapas list; the best and priciest are from Huelva.

Desserts focus on the sweet and milky. *Flan* (a sort of crème caramel) is ubiquitous, great when *casero* (home-made), but often out of a plastic tub. *Natillas* are similar but smoother and creamier, while Moorish-style pastries are also specialities of some areas.

Drink

Alcoholic drinks

In good Catholic fashion, wine is the blood of Spain. It's the standard accompaniment to meals, but also features prominently in bars. *Tinto* is red, *blanco* is white and rosé is *rosado*.

A well-regulated system of *denominaciones de origen* (DO), similar to the French *appelation d'origine contrôlée*, has lifted the quality and reputation of Spanish wines. While the daddy in terms of production and popularity is still Rioja, regions such as the Ribera del Duero, Rueda, Bierzo, Rias Baixas, Jumilla, Priorat and Valdepeñas have achieved worldwide recognition. The words *crianza*, *reserva* and *gran reserva* refer to the length and nature of the ageing process.

Andalucía produces a number of good wines: look out for the *garrido fino* and (native) *zalema* varieties, used to make the fresh whites of the Condado region in eastern Huelva province and also grown in Seville province. Recommended local wineries are: Bodegas Salado, Contreras Ruiz and El Cercado de la Era; in the Sierra Norte, La Margarita, Tierra Savia and Colonias de Galeón. As a general rule, only bars that serve food serve wine; most *pubs* and *discotecas* won't have it. *Tinto de verano* is a summery mix of red wine and club soda, while the stronger *sangría* adds healthy measures of fresh fruit and spirits to the mix. The real vinous fame of the region comes, of course, from its fortified wines: sherry, which is produced in the area around Jerez de la Frontera, has shaken off its fusty image and is now appreciated for its versatility. Crisp, bone-dry fino and manzanilla are traditionally consumed at *ferias*, and pair beautifully with *jamón* and prawns, while amontillado and oloroso are appreciated for their rich, nutty flavours. A general pairing rule is: if it swims, manzanilla or fino; if it flies, amontillado; if it runs, oloroso.

Beer is mostly lager, usually reasonably strong, fairly gassy, cold and good. Sweetish Cruzcampo from Seville is found throughout the region; other local brews include San Miguel, named after the archangel in Manila where it was founded, and brewed in Málaga, and Alhambra from Granada. A *cortada* is a half-filled glass of beer, 250 ml served in a 500 ml glass, so you can it pick up without your hand warming the liquid. A *caña* is 200 ml and is served in a small glass – people often leave the last quarter in very hot weather. (Room temperature beer? *Nunca* – never!) A *tercio* is 330 ml, and a *jarra* 500 ml; if you want a large (1 litre) bottle to share, that's a *litrona*. Craft beers are hugely popular in Seville, with several dedicated bars.

Vermut (vermouth) is a popular pre-lunch aperitif. Many bars make their own vermouth by adding various herbs and fruits and letting it sit in barrels.

After dinner it's time for a *copa*. People relax over a whisky or a brandy, or hit the *cubatas* (mixed drinks); gin and tonic, rum and coke, and whisky and coke are the most popular. Spirits are free-poured and large.

When ordering a spirit, you'll be expected to choose which brand you want; the range of gins in particular is extraordinary. Locally produced brands include Clandestina and Puerto de Indias; there's also the excellent Tanqueray Flor de Sevilla bitter orange gin, although this is made in the UK. There's always a good selection of rum (*ron*) and blended whisky available too. *Chupitos* are short drinks often served in shot glasses.

Non-alcoholic drinks

Zumo (fruit juice) is normally bottled; *mosto* (grape juice, really pre-fermented wine) is a popular soft drink in bars. All bars serve alcohol-free beer (*cerveza sin alcohol*) but be sure to check because it is sometimes 1% alcohol. *Agua* (water) comes *con* (with) or *sin* (without) *gas*. The tap water is totally safe. Many hotels and restaurants provide filtered water in reusable glass bottles.

Café (coffee) is excellent and strong. *Solo* is black, served espresso style. Order *americano* if you want a long black, *cortado* if you want a dash of milk, or *con leche* for about half milk. Nearly everywhere has non-dairy 'milk' on offer, with oat and soya being the most common. Independent specialist coffee bars abound in Seville, so you'll never have to visit Starbucks. *Té* (tea) is served without milk unless you ask – be sure to specify *leche frío aparte* (cold milk on the side), because tea is sometimes served as hot water with a teabag neatly laid next to it. Specialist tea cafés will obviously know what they're doing. Herbal teas (*infusiones*) are common, especially chamomile (*manzanilla*; not to be confused with the sherry of the same name) and mint (*menta poleo*). For soft drinks, kombucha (fermented tea) is served in a small number of bars; try Kombucha-T, made by a sevillano company. Iced tea is also widely available, along with the usual flavoured sodas.

Essentials A-Z

Accidents and emergencies

General emergencies T112.

Children

Kids are kings in Spain and it's one of the easiest places to take them along on holiday. Children socialise with their parents from an early age and you'll see them eating in restaurants and out in bars well after midnight. Outdoor summer life and pedestrianised areas of cities make for a stress-free time for both you and the kids.

Spaniards are friendly and accommodating towards children and you'll undoubtedly get treated better with them than without them, except perhaps in the most expensive restaurants and hotels. Most places are equipped with highchairs and baby-changing facilities. Children are expected to eat the same sort of things as their parents, although you'll sometimes see a *menú infantil* at a restaurant, which typically has simpler dishes and smaller portions. Spanish campsites and larger coastal hotels are well set up, the larger ones often with child-minding facilities.

The cut-off age for children paying half or being free on public transport and in tourist attractions varies widely. Renfe trains let under-4s on free and offer discounts of around 40% for 4- to 13-year-olds. Most car-rental companies have child seats available, but it's wise to book these in advance, particularly in summer.

Bear in mind that Seville can get unbearably hot in the summer.

Customs and duty free

Non-EU citizens are allowed to import 1 litre of spirits, 2 litres of wine and 200 cigarettes or 250 g of tobacco or 50 cigars. EU citizens are theoretically limited by personal use only.

Travelling with a disability

Spain isn't the best equipped of countries in terms of travelling with a disability, but things are improving rapidly. By law, all new public buildings have to have full disabled access and facilities, and disabled toilets are increasingly common elsewhere. Many beaches are accessible and have adapted toilets.

Most trains and stations are wheelchair friendly to some degree, as well as urban buses, metro and trams. **Yellow Car** at Málaga airport ⓘ *www. yellowcar.com* rents out wheelchair-adapted vehicles. Nearly all underground and municipal car parks have lifts and disabled spaces, as do many museums, castles, etc.

An invaluable resource for finding a bed are the regional accommodation lists, available from tourist offices and the www.andalucia.org website. Most of these include an 'accessible tourism' criterion. Many *hostales* are in buildings with ramps and lifts, but there are many that are not, and the lifts can be very small. Nearly all paradores and chain hotels are fully accessible by wheelchair, as is any accommodation built since 1995, but it's best to double-check when booking. Some hotels have lifts for their swimming pools.

While major cities are relatively straightforward, albeit with cobbled streets and narrow pavements, smaller towns and villages frequently have uneven footpaths, steep streets and little, if any, disabled infrastructure.

Useful contacts
Disability and Travel Abroad, www.gov.uk/government/publications/disabled-travellers, offers information for people with disabilities about travelling internationally.
Confederación Nacional de Sordos de España (CNSE), www.cnse.es, has links to local associations for people who are deaf.
Tur4all, www.tur4all.com, is a fantastic resource with a wide range of information about accessible tourism.
ONCE, www.once.es. The national organisation for people who are blind, and which runs a lucrative daily lottery, ONCE can provide information on accessible attractions for travellers with visual impairments.

Electricity

230V. A round 2-pin plug is used (European standard).

Embassies and consulates

For a list of Spanish embassies abroad, see http://embassy.goabroad.com.

Festivals and public holidays
Festivals
As well as Seville's famous Semana Santa and Feria de Abril celebrations (see boxes, pages 18 and 26), in Sep/Oct the Bienal de Flamenco is held every even-numbered year. The most respected names in flamenco perform here, with more than 600 artists taking part. Check dates at www.labienal.com.

Even the smallest village in Seville has a fiesta and many have several. Although mostly nominally religious featuring a mass and procession or two, they also offer live music, bullfights, competitions and fireworks. A feature of many are *gigantes y cabezudos*, huge-headed papier mâché figures based on historical personages who parade the streets. In many villages there's a Moros y Cristianos festival, which recreates a Reconquista battle with colourful costumes.

Most fiestas are in summer; expect some trouble finding accommodation. Details of the major town fiestas can be found in the travel text. National holidays and *puentes* (long weekends) can be difficult times to travel, so it's important to reserve tickets in advance.

Public holidays
1 Jan **Año Nuevo**, New Year's Day.
6 Jan **Reyes Magos/Epifanía**, Epiphany, when Christmas presents are given, with Three Kings processions on 5 Jan.
28 Feb **Andalucía day**.
Easter **Jueves Santo, Viernes Santo, Día de Pascua** (Maundy Thu, Good Fri, Easter Sun).
1 May **Fiesta del Trabajo** (Labour Day).
24 Jun **Fiesta de San Juan** (Feast of St John).
25 Jul **Día del Apóstol Santiago**, Feast of St James.
15 Aug **Asunción**, Feast of the Assumption.
12 Oct **Día de la Hispanidad**, Spanish National Day (Columbus Day, Feast of the Virgin of the Pillar).
1 Nov **Todos los Santos**, All Saints' Day.
6 Dec **El Día de la Constitución Española**, Constitution Day.

8 Dec **Inmaculada Concepción,** Feast of the Immaculate Conception. **25 Dec** **Navidad**, Christmas Day.

Health

Medical facilities in Seville are very good. However, UK residents should make sure they have the **European Health Insurance Card** (EHIC) or **Global Health Insurance Card** (GHIC) to prove reciprocal rights to medical care. These are available free of charge in the UK from the NHS (www.nhs.uk).

Other **non-EU citizens** should consider travel insurance to cover emergency and routine medical needs; be sure that it covers any sports or activities you may do. Check for reciprocal cover with your private or public health scheme first.

Water is safe to drink. The **sun** in southern Spain can be harsh, so take precautions to avoid heat exhaustion and sunburn.

Many medications that require a prescription in other countries are available over the counter at pharmacies in Spain. Pharmacists are highly trained and usually speak some English. In medium-sized towns and Seville city, at least one pharmacy is open 24 hrs; this is performed on a rota system (posted in the window of all pharmacies and listed on https://farmacias365.com).

No vaccinations are needed.

Insurance

Insurance is a good idea to cover you for theft or loss of valuables or documents. In the unlucky event of theft, you'll have to make a report at the local police station within 24 hrs and obtain a *denuncia* (report) to show your insurers. See above for health cover for EU citizens.

Internet

Cyber cafés are increasingly rare in Spain, though you'll still find them in Seville city. Other places that often offer access are *locutorios* (call shops), which are common in areas with a high immigrant population. Most accommodation and many cafés and restaurants offer Wi-Fi. Mobile phone providers offer pay-as-you-go data SIM cards and USB modems at a reasonable rate. Most UK mobile phone companies charge for data roaming in Spain; some have a 'fair use' data cap of 5-50GB, and/or around £40-50 – check before you leave.

Language

Everyone in Seville speaks Spanish, known either as *castellano* or *español*, and it's a huge help to know some. The local accent, *andaluz*, is characterised by dropping consonants left, right and centre, thus *dos tapas* tends to be pronounced *dotapa*. Unlike in the rest of Spain, the letters 'c' and 'z' in words such as *cerveza* aren't pronounced 'th' (although in Cádiz province, perversely, they tend to pronounce 's' with that sound).

Most young people know some English (a lower-intermediate level is necessary for any university degree), and standards are rising fast, especially in the tourism sector: pretty much all hotel, restaurant and major attraction staff will have a good level, but don't assume that other people aged 40 or over know any at all. Spaniards are often shy to attempt to speak English. Most visitor attractions have information available in English (and to a lesser extent French and German). All tourist office staff speak

English and there's a good range of translated information available in most places. People are used to speaking English in well-visited areas, but trying even a couple of words of Spanish is basic politeness (see page 110). Small courtesies grease the wheels of everyday interaction here: greet the proprietor or waiting staff when entering a shop or bar, and say *hasta luego* when leaving. See page 110 for useful words and phrases in Spanish, and box, page 49, for language schools in Seville.

LGBTQIA+ travellers

Homosexuality is legal, as is gay marriage. There are different levels of tolerance and open-mindedness towards gays and lesbians in Andalucía. In Seville there's a fairly lively gay scene around the Alameda, although not on a par with Barcelona or Madrid. In smaller places, however, it can be a different story, and a couple walking hand-in-hand will likely be greeted with incredulous stares, although rarely anything worse.

Useful contacts
COLEGA, www.colegaweb.org. A gay and lesbian association with an office in Seville.
Shangay/Shanguide, www.shangay.com, is a useful magazine with reviews, events, information and city-by-city listings for the whole country.

Useful websites
www.damron.com Subscription listings and travel info.

Media

Newspapers and magazines
The Spanish press is generally of a high journalistic standard. The national dailies, *El País* (still a qualitative leap ahead), *El Mundo* and the rightist *ABC*, are read throughout the country, but local papers are widely read in Seville. According to data company Statista, 38% of Spaniards still read the daily press. Many people read newspaper apps on their devices; some are free and some are subscription only. Each major city has its own newspaper or edition: in Seville, *Diario de Sevilla* is one of the best. There are also 'what's on' magazines, often distributed in tourist offices or bars, as well as apps listing events and attractions.

The terribly Real Madrid-biased sports dailies *Marca* and *AS*, dedicated mostly to football, have a large readership that rivals any of the broadsheets. There's no tabloid press as such; the closest equivalent is the *prensa de corazón* and gossip magazines such as *¡Hola!*, forerunner of Britain's *Hello!* Several English dailies have European editions available on the day of publication; the same goes for major European dailies. English-language local-news websites include *The Local* ⓘ www.thelocal.es and the tabloidy *Olive Press* ⓘ www.theolivepress.es.

Radio
Radio is big in Spain, with audience figures relatively higher than most of Europe. There's a huge range of stations, many of them broadcasting to a fairly small regional area. You'll be unlikely to get much exposure to it (beyond the top-40 music stations blaring in bars) unless you're in a car. RAI (Radio Andalucía Información), digital and 94.3 FM, is useful for news (in Spanish).

TV
TV is the dominant legacy medium in Spain, with audience figures well above

most of the EU. The main channels are the state-run *TVE1*, with standard programming, and *TVE2*, with a more cultural/sporting bent alongside the private *Antena 3*, *Cuatro* and *Tele 5*, and *La Sexta (6)*. Regional stations also draw audiences. Overall quality is low, with reality shows and lowest-common-denominator kitsch as popular here as anywhere. Cable TV is widespread, and satellite and digital have a wide market. As with everywhere, social media is huge, and many people of all ages watch TV and streaming services on their personal devices.

Money

Currency and exchange
For up-to-the-minute exchange rates visit www.xe.com.

The euro (€) is divided into 100 *céntimos*. Euro notes are standard across the whole euro zone and come in denominations of 5, 10, 20, 50, 100, and the rarely seen 200 and 500. Coins have one standard face and one national face; all coins are, however, acceptable in all countries. The coins are slightly difficult to tell apart when you're not used to them. The coppers are 1, 2 and 5 cent pieces, the golds are 10, 20 and 50, and the silver/gold combinations are €1 and €2.

ATMs and banks
Contactless payments are widely accepted, using both cards and mobile phones, but it's always a good idea to carry some cash. ATMs are plentiful and accept all the major international debit and credit cards. Be aware that Spanish banks charge commission when you withdraw cash from an ATM, and beware of your own bank hitting you for a hefty

fee: check with them before leaving home. Even if they do, it's likely to be a better deal than changing cash over a counter.

Banks are usually open Mon-Fri 0830-1430, and many change foreign money (sometimes only the central branch in a town will do it). Cities will also have bureaux de change, which have longer opening hours. Commission rates vary, so it's worth comparing them with banks. The website www.moneysavingexpert.com has a good run-down on the most economical ways of accessing cash, and which cards to pay with, while travelling.

Cost of living
Seville offers good value for money, and you can get by cheaply if you forego a few luxuries. If you're travelling as a pair, staying in cheap *pensiones*, eating a set meal at lunchtime, travelling short distances by bus or train daily, and snacking on tapas in the evenings, €65 per person per day is reasonable. In a good *hostal* or cheap hotel and using a car, €150 a day and you'll not be counting pennies; €300 per day and you'll be very comfy indeed unless you're staying in 5-star accommodation.

Accommodation is usually more expensive in summer than winter. Seville is noticeably pricier than elsewhere in Andalucía.

Public transport is generally cheap; intercity bus services are quick and low-priced. If you're hiring a car, Málaga is the cheapest place in Andalucía. Standard unleaded petrol is around €1.45 per litre. In some places, particularly in tourist areas, you may be charged up to 20% more to sit outside a restaurant. It's also worth checking if the 10% IVA (sales tax) is included in prices, especially in the more expensive restaurants – it should say on the menu.

Opening hours

Business hours Mon-Fri 1000-1400, 1700-2000; Sat 1000-1400. **Banks** Mon-Fri 0830-1430. **Government offices** Mornings only.

Post

The Spanish post is still somewhat slow by European standards. *Correos* (post offices) generally open Mon-Fri 0830-1430; Sat 0800-1300, although main offices in large towns will stay open all day. Stamps can be bought here or at *estancos* (tobacconists).

Safety

Seville is a very safe place to travel. There's been a crackdown on tourist crime in recent years and Seville feels much safer than a city of equivalent size in England.

What tourist crime there is tends to be of the opportunistic kind. Robberies from parked cars (particularly those with foreign plates) are not unknown, and the occasional mugger operates in Seville. If parking in Seville city or a popular hiking zone, make it clear there's nothing worth robbing in a car by leaving the glove compartment open.

If you are unfortunate enough to be robbed, you should report the theft immediately at the nearest police station, because insurance companies will require a copy of the *denuncia* (police report). The tourist police are based at Seville City Office in Marqués de Contadero, by the Torre del Oro.

Smoking

Smoking is increasingly less common in Spain, though vaping is popular. It is banned in all enclosed spaces (ie bars and restaurants), and there are plans to also make beaches, pools and outdoor terraces non-smoking areas. There are still rooms for smokers in some hotels, limited to 30%. Prices are standardised, and you can buy cigarettes at tobacconists or at machines in cafés and bars (with a small surcharge).

Student travellers

An **International Student Identity Card** or **International Youth Travel Card** (under 31 years) (ISIC; www.isic.org), for full-time students, is worth having in Spain. Get one at your place of study, or at many travel agencies both in and outside Spain. The cost varies from country to country, but is generally about €11 – a good investment, providing discounts of up to 20% on some plane fares, train tickets, museum entries, bus tickets and some accommodation.

Taxes

Nearly all goods and services in Spain are subject to a value-added tax (IVA). This is 10% for things like transport, hotels and restaurant meals, but is 21% on retail items like clothes, homeware and technology, as well as alcohol outside of restaurants. IVA is normally included in the stated prices. You're technically entitled to claim it back if you're a non-EU citizen, for purchases over €90. Pick up a DIVA form from the retailer, and validate it at the airport before you leave. You can claim the amount back at major airports on departure.

Telephone

Country code +34

Domestic landlines have 9-digit numbers beginning with 9. Although the first 3 digits indicate the province, you have to dial the full number from wherever you are calling, including abroad. Mobile numbers start with 6 or 7.

Most foreign mobiles will work in Spain: check your phone's GSM compatibility, and your network's roaming charges, before leaving. Many mobile networks require you to activate roaming (for use while abroad) on your phone before leaving your home country. If you're staying a while and have an unlocked phone, it's pretty cheap to buy a Spanish SIM card or eSIM.

Time

1 hr ahead of GMT. Clocks go forward an hour in late Mar and back in late Oct with the rest of the EU.

Tipping

Tipping in Spain is far from compulsory. A 10% tip would be considered extremely generous in a restaurant; 3% to 5% is more usual. It's rare for a service charge to be added to a bill. Waiters don't expect tips but in bars and cafés people will sometimes leave small change, especially for table service. Taxi drivers don't expect a tip, but will be pleased to receive one.

Tourist information

The tourist information infrastructure in Andalucía is organised by the Junta (the regional government) and is generally excellent, with a wide range of information, often in English, German and French as well as Spanish. The website www.andalucia.org has comprehensive information and *oficinas de turismo* (local government tourist offices) are in all the major towns, providing more specific local information. In addition, many towns run a municipal *turismo*, offering locally produced material. The tourist offices are generally open during normal office hours and in the main holiday areas normally have enthusiastic, multilingual staff. The tourist offices can provide local maps and town plans and a full list of registered accommodation. Staff are not allowed to make recommendations. If you're in a car, it's especially worth asking for a listing of *casas rurales* (rural accommodation). In villages with no *turismo* you could try asking for local information on accommodation and sights in the *ayuntamiento* (town hall).

There is a substantial amount of tourist information on the internet. Apart from the websites listed (see below), many towns and villages have their own site with information on sights, hotels and restaurants, although this may be in Spanish.

The **Spanish Tourist Board** (www.spain.info) produces a mass of information on a wide range of topics.

Useful websites

www.aemet.es Site of the national meteorological agency, with the day's weather and next-day forecasts.
www.alsa.es One of the country's main bus companies with online booking.
www.andalucia.com Excellent site with comprehensive practical and background information on Andalucía, covering everything from accommodation to zoos.

www.andalucia.org The official tourist-board site, with details of even the smallest villages, accommodation and tourist offices.

www.booking.com The most useful online accommodation booker for Spain.

www.dgt.es The transport department website has up-to-date information in Spanish on road conditions throughout the country.

www.elpais.com Online edition of Spain's biggest-selling daily paper. Also in English, www.english.elpais.com.

www.guiarepsol.com Online route planner for Spanish roads, also available in English.

www.inturjoven.com Details of youth hostel locations, facilities and prices.

maps.google.es Street maps of most Spanish towns and cities.

www,movelia.es Online timetables and ticketing for some bus companies.

www.paginasamarillas.es Yellow Pages.

www.parador.es Parador information, including locations, prices and photos.

www.raar.es Andalucian rural accommodation network with details of mainly self-catering accommodation to rent, including cottages and farmhouses.

www.renfe.com Online timetables and tickets for Renfe train network.

www.spain.info The official website of the Spanish tourist board.

www.soccer-spain.com A website in English dedicated to Spanish football.

www.ticketmaster.es Spain's biggest ticketing agency for concerts and more, with online purchase.

www.toprural.com and **www.todoturismorural.com** 2 of many sites for *casas rurales*.

www.tourspain.es A useful website run by the Spanish tourist board.

UK and Ireland

Abercrombie and Kent, www.abercrombiekent.com. Upmarket operator offering tailor-made itineraries in Andalucía as well as the rest of Spain.

ACE Cultural Tours, www.aceculturaltours.co.uk. Trips focusing on Moorish culture, as well as wildlife.

Andante Travels, www.andantetravels.com. Popular operator running a variety of different cultural and active holidays in Andalucía. It focuses on archaeology and the Roman presence.

Cycling Safaris, www.cyclingsafaris.com. Irish operator offering well-priced tours to Andalucía.

Exodus, www.exodus.co.uk. Walking and adventure tours to suit all pockets.

Martin Randall Travel, www.martinrandall.com. Excellent cultural itineraries accompanied by lectures. Covers all the main cities, and also has an offbeat tour visiting some out-of-the-way spots.

Rest of Europe

Bravo Bike Travel, www.bravobike.com. Runs 8-day bike tours of Andalucía.

North America

Cycling Through The Centuries, www.cycling-centuries.com. Runs guided cycling tours of Andalucía.

Magical Spain, www.magicalspain.com. American-run tour agency based in Seville, which runs a variety of tours.

Spain Adventures, www.spainadventures.com. Organises a range of hiking and biking tours.

Australia

Timeless Tours & Travel, www.timeless.com.au. Specialises in tailored itineraries for Spain.

Visas and immigration

EU citizens and those from Schengen countries can enter Spain freely. UK and Irish citizens will need to carry a passport, while an identity card suffices for other EU/Schengen nationals. At the time of writing, the EU's new digital border control for non-EU nationals, EES (Entry/Exit System), was being introduced, causing extra delays. It records biometric information (photo and fingerprints; data is stored for three years), as well as passport entry/exit dates and locations. The system is designed to (eventually) speed up border checks for travellers, replacing physical stamps in passports. Citizens of Australia, the USA, Canada, New Zealand, several Latin American countries and Israel can enter without a visa for up to 90 days. By April 2027 (date as of time of writing), these travellers will need an ETIAS, a visa waiver valid for three years that costs €20 (free for under-18s and over-70s). Other citizens will require a Schengen Visa, obtainable from Spanish consulates or embassies. These are usually issued quickly and are valid for all Schengen countries. The basic visa is valid for 90 days, and you'll need 2 passport photos, proof of funds covering your stay, and possibly evidence of medical cover (ie insurance).

For extensions of visas, apply to an *oficina de extranjeros* in a major city (usually in the *comisaría*, main police station).

Weights and measures

Metric.

Working in the country

The most obvious paid work for English speakers is through teaching the language. Even the smallest towns usually have an English academy or two. Rates of pay aren't great except in the large cities, but you can live quite comfortably. The best way of finding work is by trawling around the schools, but there are dozens of useful internet sites – check www.eslcafe.com for links and listings. There's also a more casual scene of private teaching: noticeboards in universities and student cafés are the best way to find work of this sort, or to advertise your own services. Standard rates for 1-to-1 classes are €15-30 per hr.

Casual bar work is also relatively easy to find, particularly in summer on the coast. Live-in English-speaking au pairs and childminders (maximum stay 3 months without a visa) are also popular with wealthier city families. The **International Au Pair Association** (www.iapa.org) lists reliable agencies that arrange placements. The online forum **Au Pair World** (www.aupairworld. com) is a popular free service.

EU citizens are at an advantage when it comes to working in Spain, because they can work without a permit.

Since Brexit, it has become more complicated for UK citizens to work in Spain. To get work in a Spanish company, such as a language academy or international school, all non-EU citizens will need a firm job offer and a temporary work visa, which the company applies for before you arrive in Spain. This takes 6-10 months to get, lasts 1 year and can be extended to five years maximum. Another option is to study Spanish and apply for a student visa, which allows you to work for 20 hours a week. UK nationals/residents can also work as a language assistant on the British Council's ELA programme.

For non-EU citizens working remotely for companies outside the country, the DNV (Digital Nomad Visa) allows these workers to live and work in Spain. Freelancers with up to 20% of income from Spanish clients can also apply for this visa.

Basic Spanish for travellers

Learning Spanish is a useful part of the preparation for a trip to Spain and no volumes of dictionaries, phrase books or word lists will provide the same enjoyment as being able to communicate directly with the people of the country you are visiting. It is a good idea to make an effort to grasp the basics before you go. As you travel you will pick up more of the language and the more you know, the more you will benefit from your stay. Regional accents and usages vary, but the basic language is essentially the same everywhere.

Vowels

a	as in English *cat*
e	as in English *best*
i	as the ee in English *feet*
o	as in English *shop*
u	as the oo in English *food*
ai	as the i in English *ride*
ei	as ey in English *they*
oi	as oy in English *toy*

Consonants

Most consonants can be pronounced more or less as they are in English. The exceptions are:

g	before *e* or *i* is the same as *j*
h	is always silent (except in *ch* as in *chair*)
j	as the *ch* in Scottish *loch*
ll	as the *y* in *yellow*
ñ	as the *ni* in English *onion*
rr	trilled much more than in English
x	depending on its location, pronounced *x*, *s*, *sh* or *j*

Spanish words and phrases

Greetings, courtesies

hello	*hola*	thank you (very much)	*(muchas) gracias*
good morning	*buenos días*		
good afternoon/evening	*buenas tardes/ noches*	I speak a little Spanish	*hablo un poco de español*
goodbye	*adiós/ hasta luego*	I don't speak Spanish	*no hablo español*
		do you speak English?	*¿hablas inglés?*
pleased to meet you	*encantado/a*	I don't understand	*no entiendo*
how are you?	*¿cómo estás?*	please speak slowly	*habla despacio por favor*
I'm called …	*me llamo …*		
what is your name?	*¿cómo te llamas?*	I am very sorry	*lo siento mucho/ discúlpame*
I'm fine, thanks	*muy bien, gracias*	what do you want?	*¿qué quieres?*
yes/no	*sí/no*	I want/would like	*quiero/quería*
		I don't want it	*no lo quiero*
please	*por favor*	good/bad	*bueno/malo*

Basic questions and requests

have you got a room for two people?		when?	¿cuándo?
¿tienes una habitación para dos		where is …?	*¿dónde está …?*
personas?		where can I buy?	*¿dónde puedo*
how do I get to …?	*¿cómo llego a …?*		*comprar …?*
how much does it cost?		where is the nearest petrol station?	
¿cuánto cuesta? ¿cuánto es?		*¿dónde está la gasolinera más cercana?*	
is VAT included?	*¿el IVA está incluido?*	why?	*¿por qué?*
when does the bus leave (arrive)?			
¿a qué hora sale (llega) el autobús?			

Basic words and phrases

bank	*el banco*	market	*el mercado*
bathroom/toilet	*el baño*	note/coin	*el billete/la moneda*
to be	*ser, estar*	police (policeman)	*la policía (el policía)*
bill	*la factura/la cuenta*	post office	*el correo*
cash	*efectivo*	public telephone	*el teléfono público*
cheap	*barato/a*	shop	*la tienda*
credit card	*la tarjeta de crédito*	supermarket	*el supermercado*
exchange rate	*el tipo de cambio*	there is/are	*hay*
expensive	*caro/a*	there isn't/aren't	*no hay*
to go	*ir*	ticket office	*la taquilla*
to have	*tener, haber*	traveller's cheques	*los cheques de viaje*

Getting around

aeroplane	*el avión*	luggage	*el equipaje*
airport	*el aeropuerto*	motorway, freeway	*el autopista/autovía*
arrival/departure	*la llegada/salida*	north/south/	*el norte, el sur,*
avenue	*la avenida*	west/east	*el oeste, el este*
border	*la frontera*	oil	*el aceite*
bus station	*la estación de*	to park	*aparcar*
	autobuses	passport	*el pasaporte*
bus	*el bus/el autobús/*	petrol/gasoline	*la gasolina*
	el camión	puncture	*el pinchazo*
corner	*la esquina*	street	*la calle*
customs	*la aduana*	that way	*por allí*
left/right	*izquierda/derecha*	this way	*por aquí*
ticket	*el billete*	tyre	*el neumático*
empty/full	*vacío/lleno*	unleaded	*sin plomo*
highway, main road	*la carretera*	waiting room	*la sala de espera*
insurance	*el seguro*	to walk	*caminar/andar*
insured person	*el asegurado/la*		
	asegurada		

Accommodation

air conditioning	*el aire acondicionado*	restaurant	*el restaurante*
		room/bedroom	*la habitación*
all-inclusive	*todo incluido*	sheets	*las sábanas*
bathroom, private	*el baño privado*	shower	*la ducha*
bed, double	*la cama matrimonial*	soap	*el jabón*
		toilet	*el inódoro*
blankets	*las mantas*	toilet paper	*el papel higiénico*
to clean	*limpiar*	towels, clean/dirty	*las toallas limpias/sucias*
dining room	*el comedor*		
hotel	*el hotel*	water, hot/cold	*el agua caliente/fría*
noisy	*ruidoso*		
pillows	*las almohadas*		

Health

aspirin	*la aspirina*	diarrhoea	*la diarrea*
blood	*la sangre*	doctor	*el médico*
chemist	*la farmacia*	fever/sweat	*la fiebre/el sudor*
condoms	*los preservativos, los condones*	pain	*el dolor*
		head	*la cabeza*
contact lenses	*los lentes de contacto*	period	*la regla*
		sanitary towels	*las toallas femeninas*
contraceptives	*los anticonceptivos*		
		stomach	*el estómago*
contraceptive pill	*la píldora anticonceptiva*		

Family

family	*la familia*	boyfriend/girlfriend	*el novio/la novia*
brother/sister	*el hermano/la hermana*	friend	*el amigo/la amiga*
daughter/son	*la hija/el hijo*	married	*casado/a*
father/mother	*el padre/la madre*	single/unmarried	*soltero/a*
husband/wife	*el esposo (marido)/la mujer*		

Months, days and time

January	*enero*	July	*julio*
February	*febrero*	August	*agosto*
March	*marzo*	September	*septiembre*
April	*abril*	October	*octubre*
May	*mayo*	November	*noviembre*
June	*junio*	December	*diciembre*

Monday	*lunes*	it's one o'clock	*es la una*
Tuesday	*martes*	it's seven o'clock	*son las siete*
Wednesday	*miércoles*	it's six twenty	*son las seis y*
Thursday	*jueves*		*veinte*
Friday	*viernes*	it's five to nine	*son las nueve*
Saturday	*sábado*		*menos cinco*
Sunday	*domingo*	in ten minutes	*en diez minutos*
at one o'clock	*a la una*	five hours	*cinco horas*
at half past two	*a las dos y media*	does it take long?	*¿tarda mucho?*
at a quarter to three	*a las tres menos*		
	cuarto		

Numbers

one	*uno*	eighteen	*dieciocho*
two	*dos*	nineteen	*diecinueve*
three	*tres*	twenty	*veinte*
four	*cuatro*	twenty-one	*veintiuno*
five	*cinco*	thirty	*treinta*
six	*seis*	forty	*cuarenta*
seven	*siete*	fifty	*cincuenta*
eight	*ocho*	sixty	*sesenta*
nine	*nueve*	seventy	*setenta*
ten	*diez*	eighty	*ochenta*
eleven	*once*	ninety	*noventa*
twelve	*doce*	hundred	*cien/ciento*
thirteen	*trece*	thousand	*mil*
fourteen	*catorce*		
fifteen	*quince*		
sixteen	*dieciséis*		
seventeen	*diecisiete*		

Food glossary

A

acedía	small wedge sole
aceite	oil; *aceite de oliva* is olive oil and *aceite de girasol* is sunflower oil
aceitunas	olives, also sometimes called *olivas*. The best kind are unripe green *manzanilla*, particularly when stuffed with anchovy, *rellenas con anchoas*
adobo	marinated fried nuggets usually of shark (*tiburón*) or dogfish (*cazón*); delicious
agua	water
aguacate	avocado
ahumado	smoked; *tabla de ahumados* is a mixed plate of smoked fish
(al) ajillo	cooked in garlic, most commonly *gambas* or *pollo*
ajo	garlic, *ajetes* are young garlic shoots, often in a *revuelto*
ajo arriero	a simple sauce of garlic, paprika and parsley
ajo blanco	a chilled garlic and almond soup, a speciality of Málaga
albóndigas	meatballs
alcachofa/ alcaucil	artichoke
alcaparras	capers
aliño	any salad marinated in vinegar, olive oil and salt; often made with egg or potato, with chopped onion, peppers and tomato
alioli	a tasty sauce made from raw garlic blended with oil and egg yolk; also called *ajoaceite*
almejas	name applied to various species of small clams, often cooked with garlic, parsley and white wine
almendra	almond
alubias	broad beans
anchoa	preserved anchovy
anchoba/ anjova	bluefish
añejo	aged (of cheeses, rums, etc)
angulas	baby eels, a delicacy that has become scarce and expensive. Far more common are *gulas*, false *angulas* made from putting processed fish through a spaghetti machine; squid ink is used for authentic colouring
anís	aniseed, commonly used to flavour biscuits and liqueurs
arroz	rice; *arroz con leche* is a sweet rice pudding
asado	roast. An *asador* is a restaurant specialising in charcoal-roasted meat and fish
atún	blue-fin tuna
azúcar	sugar

B

bacalao	salted cod, either superb or leathery
berberechos	cockles
berenjena	aubergine/eggplant
besugo	red bream
bistec	steak. *Poco hecho* is rare, *al punto* is medium rare, *regular* is medium, *muy hecho* is well done
bizcocho	sponge cake or biscuit
bocadillo/ bocata	a crusty filled roll
bogavante	lobster
bonito	atlantic bonito, a small tuna fish
boquerones	fresh anchovies, often served filleted in garlic and oil
botella	bottle
(a la) brasa	cooked on a griddle over coals
buey	ox

C

caballa	mackerel
cacahuetes	peanuts
café	coffee; *solo* is black, served espresso-style; *cortado* adds a dash of milk, *con leche* more; *americano* is a long black coffee
calamares	squid
caldereta	a stew of meat or fish usually made with sherry; *venao* (venison) is commonly used, and delicious
caldo	a thin soup
callos	tripe
caña	a glass of draught beer
cangrejo	crab; occasionally river crayfish
caracol	snail; very popular in Seville – *cabrillas*, *burgaos*, and *blanquillos* are popular varieties
caramelos	boiled sweets
carne	meat
carta	menu
casero	home-made
castañas	chestnuts
cava	sparkling wine, mostly produced in Catalunya
cazuela	a stew, often of fish or seafood
cebolla	onion
cena	dinner
centollo	spider crab
cerdo	pork
cerezas	cherries
cerveza	beer
champiñón	mushroom
chipirones	small squid, often served *en su tinta*, in its own ink, mixed with butter and garlic
choco	cuttlefish
chocolate	a popular afternoon drink; also slang for hashish
chorizo	a red sausage, versatile and of varying spiciness (*picante*)
choto	roast kid
chuleta/ chuletilla	chop
chuletón	a massive T-bone steak, often sold by weight
churrasco	barbecued meat, often ribs with a spicy sauce
churro	a fried dough-stick usually eaten with hot chocolate (*chocolate con churros*). Usually eaten as a late afternoon snack (*merienda*), but sometimes for breakfast

cigala	Dublin Bay prawn/ Norway lobster
ciruela	plum
cochinillo	suckling pig
cocido	a heavy stew, usually of meat and chickpeas/beans; *sopa de cocido* is the broth
codorniz	quail
cogollo	lettuce heart
comida	lunch
conejo	rabbit
congrio	conger eel
cordero	lamb
costillas	ribs
crema catalana	a lemony crème brûlée
criadillas	hog or bull testicles
croquetas	deep-fried crumbed balls of meat, béchamel, seafood, or vegetables
cuchara	spoon
cuchillo	knife
(la) cuenta	the bill

D

desayuno	breakfast
dorada	a species of bream (gilthead)
dulce	sweet

E

ecológico	organic
embutido	any salami-type sausage
empanada	a pie, pasty-like (*empanadilla*) or in large flat tins and sold by the slice; *atun* or *bonito* is a common filling, as is ham, mince or seafood
ensalada	salad; *mixta* is usually a large serving of a bit of everything; excellent option

ensaladilla rusa	Russian salad, with potato, peas and carrots in mayonnaise
escabeche	pickled in wine and vinegar
espárragos	asparagus, white and usually canned
espinacas	spinach
estofado	braised, often in stew form

F

fabada	the most famous of Asturian dishes, a hearty stew of beans, *chorizo* and *morcilla*
fideuá	a bit like a paella but with noodles
filete	steak
fino	the classic dry sherry
flamenquín	a fried and crumbed finger of meat stuffed with ham
flan	the ubiquitous crème caramel, great when home-made (*casero*), awful when it's not
foie	fattened goose liver; often made into a thick gravy sauce
frambuesas	raspberries
fresas	strawberries
frito/a	deep-fried
fruta	fruit

G

galletas	biscuits
gallo	rooster, also the flatfish megrim
gambas	prawns
garbanzos	chickpeas, often served in *espinacas con garbanzos*, a spicy spinach dish that is a signature of Seville
gazpacho	a cold garlicky tomato soup, very refreshing

granizado	popular summer drink, like a frappé fruit milkshake
guisado/ guiso	stewed/a stew
guisantes	peas

H

habas	broad beans, often deliciously stewed *con jamón*, with ham
harina	flour
helado	ice cream
hígado	liver
higo	fig
hojaldre	puff pastry
(al) horno	oven (baked)
hueva	fish roe
huevo	egg

I/J

ibérico	see *jamón*, the term can also refer to other pork products
infusión	herbal tea
jabalí	wild boar
jamón	ham; *jamón York* is cooked British-style ham. Far better is cured *jamón serrano*; *ibérico* ham comes from Iberian pigs in western Spain fed on acorns (*bellotas*). Some places, like Jabugo, are famous for their hams, which can be expensive
(al) jerez	cooked in sherry
judías verdes	green beans

L

langosta	crayfish
langostinos	king prawns
lechazo	milk-fed lamb
leche	milk

lechuga	lettuce
lengua	tongue
lenguado	sole
lentejas	lentils
limón	lemon
lomo	loin, usually sliced pork, sometimes tuna
lubina	sea bass

M

macedonia de frutas	fruit salad, usually tinned
manchego	Spain's national cheese; hard, whitish and made from ewe's milk
manitas (de cerdo)	pork trotters
mantequilla	butter
manzana	apple
manzanilla	the dry, salty sherry from Sanlúcar de Barrameda; also, confusingly, chamomile tea and the tastiest type of olive
marisco	shellfish
mejillones	mussels
melocotón	peach, usually canned and served in *almíbar* (syrup)
melva	frigate mackerel, often served tinned or semi-dried
menestra	a vegetable stew, usually served like a minestrone without the liquid; vegetarians will be annoyed to find that it's often seeded with ham and bits of pork
menú	a set meal, usually consisting of three or more courses, bread and wine or water

menudo	tripe stew, usually with chickpeas and mint
merluza	hake is to Spain as rice is to southeast Asia
mero	grouper
miel	honey
migas	breadcrumbs, fried and often mixed with lard and meat to form a delicious rural dish of the same name
Mojama	salt-cured tuna, most common in Cádiz province
mollejas	sweetbreads; ie the pancreas of a calf or lamb
montadito	a small toasted filled roll
morcilla	blood sausage, either solid or semi-liquid
morro	cheek, pork or lamb
mostaza	mustard
mosto	grape juice; can also refer to a young wine, from 3 months old

N

naranja	orange
nata	sweet whipped cream
natillas	rich custard dessert
navajas	razor shells
nécora	small sea crab, sometimes called a velvet crab
nueces	walnuts

O

orejas	ears, usually of a pig
orujo	a fiery grape spirit, often brought to add to black coffee if the waiter likes you
ostras	oysters, also a common expression of dismay

P

paella	rice dish with saffron, seafood and/or meat
pan	bread

parrilla	grill; a parrillada is a mixed grill
pastel	cake/pastry
patatas	potatoes; often chips (patatas fritas, which confusingly can also refer to crisps); bravas are with a spicy tomato sauce
pato	duck
pavía	a crumbed and fried nugget of fish, usually bacalao or merluza
pavo	turkey
pechuga	breast (usually chicken)
perdiz	partridge
pescado	fish
pescaíto frito	Andalucian deep-fried fish and seafood
pestiños	an Arabic-style confection of pastry and honey, traditionally eaten during Semana Santa
pez espada	swordfish; delicious; sometimes called emperador
picadillo	a dish of spicy mincemeat
picante	hot, ie spicy
pichón	squab
pijota	whiting
pimienta	pepper
pimientos	peppers; there are many kinds, piquillos are the trademark thin Basque red pepper; Padrón produces sweet green mini ones. A popular tapa is pimientos aliñados (marinated roasted peppers, often with onion, sometimes with tuna)

pincho	a small snack or grilled meat on a skewer (or *pinchito*)	raya	any of a variety of rays and skates
pipas	sunflower seeds, a common snack	rebujito	a weak mix of *manzanilla* and lemonade, consumed by the bucketload during Andalucian festivals
pisto	a ratatouille-like vegetable concoction		
(a la) plancha	grilled on a hot iron or pan-fried	relleno/a	stuffed
plátano	banana	reserva, gran reserva, crianza	terms relating to the age of wines; *gran reserva* is the oldest and finest, then *reserva* followed by *crianza*
pluma	a cut of pork next to the loin		
pollo	chicken		
postre	dessert	revuelto	scrambled eggs, usually with wild mushrooms (*setas*) or seafood; often a speciality
potaje	a soup or stew		
pringá	a tasty paste of stewed meats usually eaten in a *montadito* and a traditional final tapa of the evening		
		riñones	kidneys
		rodaballo	turbot; pricey and delicious
puerros	leeks	(a la) romana	fried in batter
pulpo	octopus, particularly delicious *a la gallega*, boiled Galician style and garnished with olive oil, salt and paprika	rosca	a large round dish, a cross between sandwich and pizza
		rosquilla	doughnut
puntillitas	small squid, often served crumbed and deep fried	**S**	
		sal	salt
		salchicha	sausage
Q/R		salchichón	a salami-like sausage
queso	cheese; *de cabra* (goat's), *oveja* (sheep's) or *vaca* (cow's). It comes fresh (*fresco*), medium (*semi-curado*) or strong (*curado*)	salmón	salmon
		salmonete	red mullet
		salmorejo	a delicious thicker version of gazpacho, often garnished with egg and cured ham
rabo de buey/toro	oxtail		
ración	a portion of food served in cafés and bars; check the size and order a half (*media*) if you want less	salpicón	a seafood salad with plenty of onion and vinegar
		salsa	sauce
		San Jacobo	a steak cooked with ham and cheese
rana	frog; *ancas de rana* is frogs' legs	sandía	watermelon
rape	monkfish/anglerfish	sardinas	sardines, delicious grilled

sargo	white sea bream
seco	dry
secreto	a cut of pork loin
sepia	cuttlefish
serrano	see *jamón*
setas	wild mushrooms, often superb
sidra	cider
solomillo	beef or pork steak cut from the sirloin bone, deliciously fried in whisky and garlic in Seville (*solomillo al whisky*)
sopa	soup; *sopa castellana* is a broth with a fried egg, noodles, and bits of ham

T

tapa	a saucer-sized portion of bar food
tarta	tart or cake
té	tea
tenedor	fork
ternera	veal or young beef
tinto	red wine is *vino tinto*; a *tinto de verano* is mixed with lemonade and ice, a refreshing option
tocino	pork lard; *tocinillo de cielo* is a caramelised egg dessert

tomate	tomato
torrijas	a Semana Santa dessert, bread fried in milk and covered in honey and cinnamon
tortilla	a Spanish omelette, with potato, egg, olive oil and optional onion; *tortilla francesa* is a French omelette
tostada	toasted, also a toasted breakfast roll eaten with olive oil, tomato or pâté
trucha	trout

U/V

uva	grape
vaso	glass
venado/venao	venison
verduras	vegetables
vieiras	scallops, also called *veneras*
vino	wine; *blanco* is white, *rosado* or *clarete* is rosé, *tinto* is red

Z

zanahoria	carrot
zumo	fruit juice, usually bottled and pricey

Glossary of architectural terms

A

alcázar   a Moorish fort

ambulatory   a gallery round the chancel and behind the altar

apse   vaulted square or rounded recess at the back of a church

archivolt   decorative carving around the outer surface of an arch

Art Deco   a style that evolved between the World Wars, based on geometric forms

artesonado ceiling   ceiling of carved wooden panels with Islamic motifs popular throughout Spain in the 15th and 16th centuries

ayuntamiento   a town hall

azulejo   an ornamental ceramic tile

B

Baldacchino   an ornate carved canopy above an altar or tomb

Baroque   ornate architectural style of the 17th and 18th centuries

bodega   a cellar where wine is kept or made; the term also refers to modern wineries and wine shops

buttress   a pillar built into a wall to reinforce areas of greatest stress. A flying buttress is set away from the wall; a feature of Gothic architecture

C

capilla   a chapel within a church or cathedral

capital   the top of column, joining it to another section. Often highly decorated

castillo   a castle or fort

catedral   a cathedral, ie the seat of a bishop

chancel   the area of a church which contains the main altar, usually at the eastern end

chapter-house   area reserved for Bible study in monastery or church

Churrigueresque   a particularly ornate form of Spanish Baroque, named after the Churriguera brothers

colegiata   a collegiate church, ie one ruled by a chapter of canons

conjunto histórico   a tourist-board term referring to an area of historic buildings

convento	a monastery or convent
coro	the area enclosing the choir stalls, often central and completely closed off in Spanish churches
crossing	the centre of a church, where the 'arms' of the cross join

E

ermita	a hermitage or rural chapel

G

Gothic	13th- to 15th-century style formerly known as pointed style; distinguished externally by pinnacles and tracery around windows, Gothic architecture lays stress on the presence of light

H

hospital	in pilgrimage terms, a place where pilgrims used to be able to rest, receive nourishment and receive medical attention

I

iglesia	a church

L

lobed arch	Moorish arch with depressions in the shape of simple arches
lonja	a guildhall or fish market

M

mocárabes	small concave spaces used as a decorative feature on Moorish ceilings and archways
modernista	a particularly imaginative variant of art nouveau that came out of Catalonia; exemplified by Gaudí
monasterio	a large monastery usually located in a rural area
monstrance	a ceremonial container for displaying the host
Mozarabic	the style of Christian artisans living under Moorish rule
mudéjar	the work of Muslims living under Christian rule after the Reconquest, characterised by ornate brickwork
multifoil	a type of Muslim-influenced arch with consecutive circular depressions
muralla	a city wall

N

nave	the main body of the church, a single or multiple passageway leading (usually) from the western end up to the crossing or high altar
neoclassical	a reaction against the excesses of Spanish Baroque, this 18th- and 19th-century style saw clean lines and symmetry valued above all things

P

palacio a palace or large residence

patio an interior courtyard

pediment triangular section between top of columns and gables

pilaster pillar attached to the wall

Plateresque derived from *platero* (silversmith); used to describe a Spanish Renaissance style characterised by finely carved decoration

R

reliquary a container to hold bones or remains of saints and other holy things

Renaissance Spanish Renaissance architecture began when classical motifs were used in combination with Gothic elements in the 16th century

retablo altarpiece or retable formed by many panels often rising to roof level; can be painted or sculptured

Romanesque (románico) style spread from France in the 11th and 12th centuries, characterised by barrel vaulting, rounded apses and semicircular arches

Romano Roman

S

sacristy (sacristía) part of church reserved for priests to prepare for services

soportales wooden or stone supports for the 1st floor of civic buildings, forming an arcade underneath

stucco (yesería) moulding mix consisting mainly of plaster; fundamental part of Moorish architecture

Index

*Entries in **bold** refer to maps*

FOOTPRINT
Features

Credits

Fourth edition published June 2026
First published by Footprint handbooks and written by Andy Symington

Bradt Travel Guides Ltd
31a High Street, Chesham, Buckinghamshire, HP5 1BW, England
www.bradtguides.com
Print edition published in the USA by The Globe Pequot Press Inc, PO Box 480, Guilford, Connecticut 06437-0480

Thank you for buying an authorised edition of this book published by Bradt Travel Guides. For over 50 years, Bradt Travel Guides has encouraged adventurous, immersive and responsible travel, and this is only possible because of the support of our readers. By purchasing our books, you are enabling us to continue to commission expert authors who genuinely know and love the places they write about, and who write their books after thorough, on-the-ground research.

ISBN: 9781804693896

British Library Cataloguing in Publication Data
A catalogue record for this book is available from the British Library

Importer to the EU: Freytag-Berndt u. Artaria KG, Ölzeltgasse 3/10, 1030 Wien, Österreich

Photographs AWL Images (AWL); Shutterstock.com (S)
Front cover Las Setas at Dusk (Neil Farrin/AWL)
Inside front cover Alcázar Gardens (Mistervlad/S); Tiles on the Royal Tobacco Factory (Virginia Marin/S); Butcher cutting meat in Triana Market (O.Kemppainen/S)
Back cover Top left: Las Teresas bar (Kevin Hellon/S); right: Torre del Oro (Mistervlad/S); below left: Plaza Cabildo (LucVi/S)
Title page Casa de Pilatos (Marco Taliani de Marchio/S); Oranges growing in the city centre (Melanie Hobson/S); Andalucian *azulejos* are prevalent on buildings across the city (joserpizarro/S); Women in colourful dresses at the Feria (Javidestock/S)
Colour section pages 2–3: Neirfy/S; page 4: Maria Albi/S, Art_Gants/S, Karol Kozlowski/S; page 5: ColorMaker/S, Tupungato/S, Irina WS/S, Achim Wagner/S; page 7: Ana Iacob Photography/S, julia.mlozano/S, Richard Semik/S; page 8: Alina Fomenko/S

Maps David McCutcheon FBCart.S. FRGS assisted by Pearl Geo Solutions
Typeset by BBR Design
Production managed by Imprint Press; printed in India
Digital conversion by www.dataworks.co.in